EAST MEETS WEST

EAST MEETS WEST

GLOBAL DESIGN FOR CONTEMPORARY INTERIORS

KELLY HOPPEN

SPECIAL PHOTOGRAPHY BY BILL BATTEN

FOREWORD BY DAVID TANG

TEXT BY ALEXANDRA CAMPBELL

conran
OCTOPUS

First published in 1997 by

Conran Octopus Limited

a part of Octopus Publishing Group

2-4 Heron Quays, London E14 4JP

This paperback edition published in 2001

Reprinted in 2003

Commissioning Editor: Denny Hemming

Copy Editor: Paula Hardy

Art Directors: Karen Bowen and Helen Lewis

Designer: Karen Bowen

Picture Researcher: Clare Limpus

Production Controller: Julia Golding

British Library Cataloguing-in-Publication Data

A catalogue record for this book is available from the
British Library

ISBN 1 84091 179 4

Printed in China

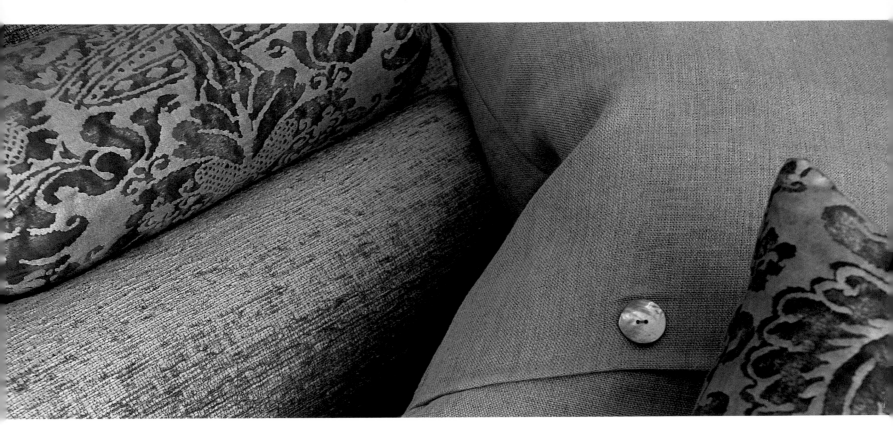

CONTENTS

I suppose it was prophets and profits that first linked the East and the West: the great Silk Route along which travelled the teachings of Buddha, Mohammed and Christ, and the caravans which exchanged precious metals for silks; the epic sea voyages by the Dutch, Portuguese and the Spaniards in search of spices from Java; and the East India Company's trade with China in tea and porcelain and eventually opium. However, not many Occidentals managed to reach the Orient, which remained a mystery for centuries to come. What little knowledge there was of the East came from famous travellers like Marco Polo, Friar Odoric and Matteo Ricci. On the whole, it was the Western imagination that remained the most fertile ground for Eastern exoticism.

It was not until the seventeenth century that the Dutch despatched an embassy to Peking, hoping to establish both diplomatic and trade connections. Although this mission was frustrated, the steward to the Dutch ambassador, one Johan Nieuwhoff, turned out to be an excellent draftsman and compiled a collection of drawings – including views of the porcelain tower of Nanking and the Imperial gardens at Peking – which he brought back to Europe. His illustrations showed, for the first time, what China was really like, and his published engravings soon became an inspiration for chinoiserie – a European style inspired by the East.

Since then, there has been no looking back. Today, with the magic of travel, the border between East and West has almost disappeared. But it would be a great pity if the spirit of East meeting West were to be taken for granted, because it is still possible for exoticism to remain even after all these years of exploration and mutual influences.

In this respect, Kelly Hoppen has produced a beautiful and spiritual book on the juxtaposition of Eastern and Western style. There is no greater manifestation of modern living, nor one that impinges on our lives more, than interior design, and I am sure that this volume will awaken the reader to the great cross-culture between the East and the West, the *yin* and the *yang*.

It might have taken prophets and profits, and almost a millennium, to synthesize this meeting between the two hemispheres, but the artistry produced by the combination of East and West will go on flourishing for a long time yet. *East Meets West* is a testament to that.

David Tang

FOREWORD

Global travel has had an extraordinary impact on all our lives, and nowhere is this more evident than in the arenas of fashion and design. Throughout the ages, artists have been inspired by the exotic and unusual and have strived in their work to harmonize and balance the different elements that make up the world we live in. Harmony has to be the key word for an interior designer, and as our lives become more cosmopolitan so should our homes. My fascination with Eastern style has arisen from this need. For me East meets West is a truly modern look. It is contemporary and yet it values traditional skills and workmanship, it is flexible and thus reflects the nature of a modern life-style, and it is highly individual, always incorporating an original twist.

I have been designing interiors over the last twenty years, gathering inspiration from my travels all over the world. Whether my ideas come from food, fashion, music, architecture or art – I never stop creating, it's a passion. Rather than dictate a particular style to my clients, I see myself in the role of an interpreter. I need to get inside a client's head and discover their personality before I can guide them towards a style, a look, an atmosphere in which they will want to live. It is absolutely essential to give people the home that they want. You must invest a house with character; it should be inviting yet functional, uncluttered yet not too minimalist – it is essential to retain the things that make a place feel like a home.

It is the mixing of textures, colours, styles and cultures that is the essence of contemporary design – nothing should be static. You need to change the style and move the contents of your home around in the same way that the Chinese rearrange their possessions; it gives a fresh feeling to your space. My reward comes when I hand people back their houses and they tell me that they feel as though they have lived there for years.

For me a room is never complete without an Eastern sense of balance. There is something about the Eastern love of simplicity and order that, when mixed with the best of contemporary Western design, is decidedly modern – it is what completes my interiors. As our lives grow more complex, this sense of simplicity and balance becomes ever more important; when we enter our homes they should not only look good, they should feel good, too.

INTRODUCTION

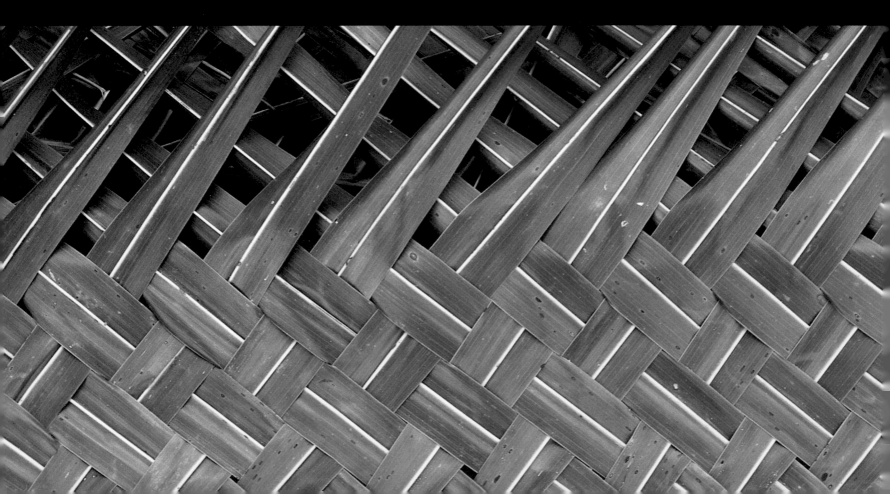

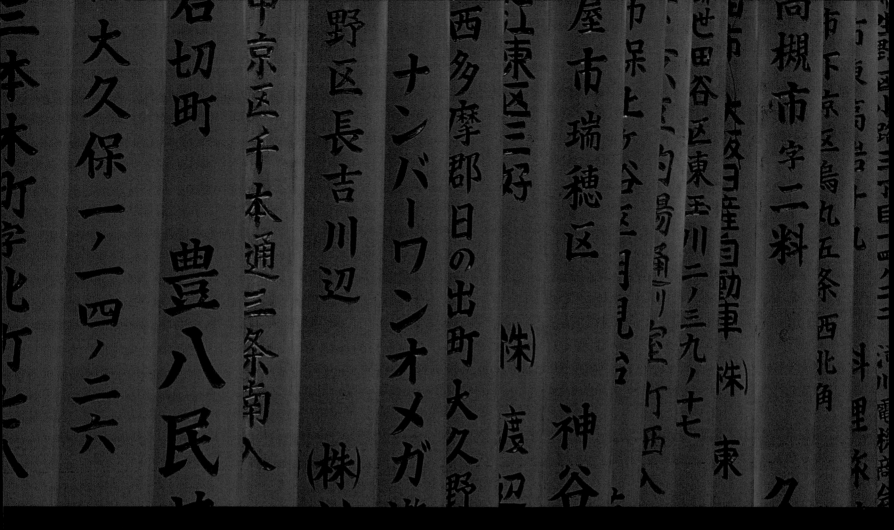

THE STYLE

INSPIRATIONS

A home decorated in East meets West style looks at first glance as though it could belong to an art collector or an explorer. Yet there is a tranquillity, and a love of clear colour and subtle texture, that can only be of today, contemporary sensibilities that hold together an accumulation of fascinating artefacts, a distillation of influences from both East and West. It is a home where contradictions work beautifully together: luxurious fabrics are used alongside combinations of humble honey-coloured coir, loose-weave linen and lining materials; and although there are objects, paintings and possessions, an oriental sense of order and calm pervades, rather than an impression of clutter.

It is a style of decoration that has as its inspiration travels to far-away places – Vietnam and Burma, India and Africa. Global travel is now a major influence on interior design, and there is a new momentum to this melding of Eastern and Western cultures, as every nation is faced with the challenge of retaining their own heritage in an international age. East-West style is not a one-way trade, nor is it the imposition of one style onto another tradition. It is the result of the immeasurable exchange of cultures which now travels faster than the speed of light in images thrown from one continent to another via satellite airwaves. Changing attitudes and different tastes are propelled around the world in a way that previous generations could not have imagined. Whether in London, Paris or New York, in Tokyo, Delhi or Saigon, designers are searching for styles that connect with the past, yet are fitted for the future.

INSPIRATIONS

松濤

芳台漁書

IN THIS STRIKING DINING ROOM, KELLY HOPPEN
MAJORS IN JUST TWO COLOURS: THE LUMINOUS
DARK GREEN OF A PADDY FIELD AND A DEEP VELVETY
BLACK AGAINST A NEUTRAL BACKGROUND.
SHE ANCHORS THE THEME BY USING BLACK AS A
COMMON DENOMINATOR THROUGHOUT THE
ROOM – IN THE LAMP, IN THE CALLIGRAPHY
AND IN THE MIRROR FRAME. FINALLY, TOUCHES
OF GOLD ARE ADDED TO LIFT AND LIGHTEN.
BY USING COLOURS BOLDLY IN LARGE
BLOCKS, AND BY AVOIDING THE TEMPTATION TO
INTRODUCE ANY OTHER ELEMENTS, SHE SHOWS
HOW TRADITIONAL COLOUR COMBINATIONS
CAN LOOK STYLISHLY CONTEMPORARY.
EVEN THE GREENERY – FRESHLY CUT BAMBOO
STEMS – REFLECTS THE ATMOSPHERE: CALM,
CONTROLLED AND GEOMETRIC.

KELLY HOPPEN EVOKES THE ROUGH WEAVE OF
ROLLED MATS FROM XINGIANG, CHINA, AND
A CALLIGRAPHIC INSCRIPTION FROM THE
SULEIMAN MOSQUE, ISTANBUL (BELOW), WITH A
GIANT CHINESE SCREEN AND JUTE CARPETING IN
A ROOM WHERE TEXTURE REPLACES COLOUR
AS THE LANGUAGE OF DESIGN. THE MONOCHROME
CALLIGRAPHY DOMINATES THE SCENE WHILE
THE WHOLE ROOM IS PRESIDED OVER BY THE
INSCRUTABLE, BRONZE FEATURES OF A
LIFE-SIZE BUDDHA.

Yet such exchanges are not new in themselves. From as far back as medieval times, travellers have returned from the East to their homes in the West, bringing back beautiful objects and with their eyes opened to the simplicity and philosophy of Eastern culture. For centuries, one has been linked to the other through ancient trade routes, each culture influencing the other, with the islands of Indonesia at the crossroads. China opened up to the West in the eighteenth century, when chinoiserie became fashionable in Britain and France through blue-and-white porcelain and lacquered chests. Similarly, Japan has been influenced by China since the 1400s, and Sino-Japanese trade set the tone of its culture intensively from the Middle Ages onwards. The Portuguese reached Japan in the 1540s, followed by the Spanish and then the Dutch. India, too, has been successively influenced by the Moghuls and by contact with Chinese, Portuguese, Spanish and British cultures. The explosion of the Renaissance saw Western Europe move from medieval to modern with the discovery of new horizons and new knowledge, a development that made its influence felt throughout all aspects of civilized life. And in the melting pots of cities like Venice and Istanbul, you can see both oriental and occidental influences in glorious kilims and carpets, ceramics and calligraphy, embroidery and glassware.

It may seem something of a generalization to sweep the lands of Asia into a cultural whole – from the teeming cities of China, the secretive fastnesses of Tibet and Burma, and the ordered islands of Japan to the exuberance of India and the rich traditions of what was once Persia – but a pervading sense of exoticism can be felt throughout these lands, a distinctly 'Eastern' feel that can be sketched with broad brushstrokes. The various arms of Buddhism reach out throughout the region, instilling a love of order and harmony, a respect for craftsmanship and natural materials, and an ideal of balance between opposites, of *yin* and *yang*, female and male, dark and light, cold and warm, round and straight. All these Eastern cultures are underpinned by traditions of simplicity and discipline; the visual sense is honoured and spirituality is conveyed through the way the humblest objects are arranged.

Travel and people, sights, sounds and smells all provide inspiration for East-West interiors, as does landscape and the natural world. Patches of brilliant green rice fields bordered by sluices of running water, layers of indigo mountains, a walk on the seashore, the shimmering heat haze of high summer, the colours of an old fishing boat weathered by years of sun and wind – all of these can form a starting point for a decorative scheme. Smooth

INSPIRATIONS

KELLY HOPPEN COORDINATES A TINY SITTING
ROOM WITH A COLOUR SCHEME BASED ON
SHADES OF TERRACOTTA, CREAM AND BLACK.
THESE COLOURS HAVE BEEN INSPIRED BY A
RANGE OF CULTURAL INFLUENCES AS SEEN IN THE
OIL JARS AND A ROW OF BOOK SPINES IN A
JAPANESE SHOP. HOPPEN ALSO BORROWS THE
CONCEPT OF THE DIVAN FROM THE TURKISH *SOFA*
(RECEPTION ROOM). CONVENTIONAL FURNITURE
WOULD HAVE LOOKED MORE CLUTTERED AND
OFFERED FEWER OPTIONS.

pebbles found on a beach can come inside and be used to decorate an interior, or a piece of driftwood washed up on the shore can inspire the use of natural textures. The shape of window awnings seen in St Mark's Square, Venice, although made from humble materials such as calico and string, have an elegance and simplicity that lends itself to interior window treatments; the striped poles that mark the moorings along the Venetian canals can reappear as four-poster bed posts, decorated with twisted ribbon. Canopy beds look back to the Ottoman Empire, as does the concept of the *sofa* – originally a central reception room in the *yalis* or palaces of Istanbul, with one or two giant divans flanking the walls as virtually the only furniture in the room. Piled high with cushions and bolsters, these are not only functional but can be a prepossessing feature in a room when covered in bold fabrics. Slatted grilles, shutters and window screens – from the lacy *jalis*, or pierced wooden screens, of India to the *shoji*, or rice-paper screens, of Japan – grace homes across the two continents, demonstrating an Eastern love of ordered symmetry.

Travelling back in time offers a rich store of inspiration, a mixture of the opulent and the simple. Historical details can be adapted to offer a different slant on the contemporary interior. Medieval palaces, for all their grandeur, had few unnecessary fripperies. As in Eastern societies, furniture was kept to a minimum with chairs reserved only for the king or the gentry, long tables and benches for eating, tapestries that kept freezing rooms warm in the winter – and very little else except for sumptuous beds, draped with hangings. Design inspiration can come from just such historical detail; even medieval jousting flags, their rich velvet sewn with squares of heraldic colours, can be given a contemporary twist.

Films and books are an essential part of a country's heritage and they lead you on a different kind of journey, one that fires the imagination and conjures up images from the past, or takes you to places that you would never otherwise know. In these images of a particular culture, recorded for posterity in written works and visual images, a country's characteristics may be exaggerated for dramatic effect, but they still give us a wealth of information about dress, food, colours and fabric. Even the shape and texture of peasant or period dress can be a catalyst for using textiles in a different way, perhaps adapted as furnishing fabrics – the *obi* sash of a kimono can spark off an idea such as wrapping a strip of richly embroidered fabric around a chair as a decorative highlight.

In fact, interiors and fashion are both ways of expressing personal style and need not be seen as different disciplines. The catwalks can provide inspiration for new looks, shapes

INSPIRATIONS

A DOORWAY IN SIDI-BOU-SAID, TUNISIA, AND THE CANDY-TWIST POLES THAT MARK A MOORING ON A VENETIAN CANAL BOTH TESTIFY TO THE UNIVERSAL APPEAL OF STRIPES, COMBINING FRESHNESS AND ELEGANCE. HOPPEN TAKES THE VENETIAN MOORINGS AND RECREATES THEM IN A BOLD BLUE AND WHITE FABRIC FOR THE UPRIGHTS OF A FOUR-POSTER BED. THE SMALL SIZE OF THIS BEDROOM PRECLUDES THE USE OF A CONVENTIONAL FOUR-POSTER WITH ITS SWATHES OF FABRIC. IN THIS CASE, HOPPEN CREATES AN ILLUSION OF HEIGHT BY DRAWING THE EYE UP TO A SIMPLE STRIPED CANOPY, WHICH HAS BEEN MADE OUT OF A SINGLE BOLT OF FABRIC. THE BED BECOMES THE SINGLE STRIKING ELEMENT IN AN OTHERWISE NEUTRAL ROOM.

and ways of mixing elements. From the classic couture designs of Dior to those of Issey Miyake, whose pleated fabrics are an essay in simplicity, or Amanda Wakely with her sumptuous silk and satin evening gowns that drape so beautifully – here are ideas for using fabric or combining colours which can be translated into home furnishings. Azzedine Alaia's spare, sculptural style has an aesthetic which sits as well in the contemporary home as on a woman's body. Constantly experimenting with new materials, and making maximum use of texture in his designs, he is renowned for his use of stretch fabric, for clothes that cling and curve round the body in one sensuous movement. It is a style that makes the most of shape, and of subtle half-tones of natural colour, such as silvery greys, parchment creams and spice browns, which translate perfectly into the principles of the East meets West interior.

East-West style embraces a broad sweep of decorative influence that bridges continents and spans the millennia in terms of time: it is a blending of eras, cultures and styles rather than the uniform recreation of the look of a particular country. This design philosophy can best be described as eclectic, summed up by the juxtaposition of the treasured and handcrafted with humbler, everyday objects. It is also a very individual

INSPIRATIONS

THE ORNATE, GATHERED CALICO CANOPIES
THAT ADORN THE ARCHES OF ST MARK'S
SQUARE, VENICE, AND TRADITIONAL ARCHES
IN SEVILLE ARE RECREATED BY HOPPEN IN A
VICTORIAN STAIRWAY. THIS GIVES AN AWKWARD
WINDOW A TOUCH OF EXOTICISM.

look because everyone, in a sense, is a traveller and the homes that we return to are reflections of the lives we lead and our personalities. This is a decorating style that will work anywhere. It exudes a passion for all things oriental which are then blended within a Western context in an utterly harmonious way. Although interiors should always be constructed with an eye to function and the necesssities of everyday life, they should also reflect a careful consideration for colour, shape, space and simplicity. In this way, East-West style can convey a very personal sensibility.

Clean-lined and contemporary, simple yet exotic: these are the trademarks of this particular form of interior decoration. Yet there is more to this style than merely borrowing decorative objects from around the world and amalgamating them in a Western home. Colours and textures can be even more effective in creating a mood than objects, and the simplest of sights can provide an idea to be adapted somewhere else. Three women in saris walking to prayer along a dusty road might inspire you to combine a brilliant silk fabric against a matt, parchment-coloured wall; the crumbling grandeur glimpsed as you walk past the open doorway of an Italian palazzo might offer inspiration for wall treatments that will give depth and tone to the bland walls of a city apartment; whilst the gilded walls of a Burmese temple might inspire a silvered metallic finish for a door, skirting board, or a mirror frame.

Design in any culture can be seen in every walk of life – not only in the architecture and interiors, but also in the grid of the street layout, the everyday clothing that people wear, the china found in the humblest eating places, even the way the women in the markets lay out their produce for sale. An armful of flowers, casually gathered together at a street corner stall, can inspire a colour scheme; an inlaid marble floor in an old Turkish *hammam* or steam room, or the skilfully married reds, ochres and creams of a Persian kilim, can be re-worked in a domestic Western setting.

The most everyday object or small trinket can spur the imagination and suggest ways in which it might be used in a different and more unusual context. The ties on Japanese storage boxes, for example, with their thick knots of fabric, might be the starting point for an innovative way of securing a rolled-up window blind – and that one detail is what lends a plain blind, which could belong anywhere, an Eastern feel. Alternatively, giant storage jars from a Vietnamese market can be turned into side tables and their shape repeated around the room, in smaller jars, for a sense of unity.

JAPANESE LATTICEWORK (ABOVE CENTRE) CAN BE TRANSLATED IN SEVERAL WAYS: EITHER BY USING THE SLATTED WOOD THEME DIRECTLY (TOP), OR BY RECREATING THE IDEA IN A MORE OPEN DESIGN USING CHICKEN WIRE, WHICH HAS BEEN SPRAYED WITH GOLD PAINT (BOTTOM).

INSPIRATIONS

THE DESIGN OF THIS DOOR IN KENYA (ABOVE) HAS
ARABIC ORIGINS AND SHOWS HOW DECORATIVE
INFLUENCES HAVE TRAVELLED ACROSS CONTINENTS
FOR CENTURIES. ECHOES OF ITS CARVED
FLORAL BORDER CAN BE FOUND IN THE ORNATE
FRAMES OF THESE TWO HIGHLY DECORATED
MIRRORS, USED BY KELLY HOPPEN AS THE FOCUS
OF TWO STILL-LIFE DISPLAYS. ALTHOUGH
BOTH HAVE A BAROQUE FEEL TO THEM, THE
COMPOSITIONS REMAIN RESTRAINED. EACH STILL-
LIFE USES A LIMITED RANGE OF COLOURS, THUS
ALLOWING THE EYE TO CONCENTRATE ON THE
QUALITY OF THE WORKMANSHIP IN THE CARVING
OF THE FRAMES. THE SYMMETRICAL GROUPING OF
OBJECTS IN THE FOREGROUND ALSO LENDS TO THE
FEELING OF HARMONY AND ORDER.

Even the way a country or a culture presents its food can be an inspiration to the interior designer. The ordered, beautifully stylized dishes of Japan balance shape and colour with care, arranging garnishes and relishes to maximise their appeal to both the taste buds and the visual senses. And there is a lesson in these small compositions for anyone who sets out to arrange a group of objects. In the West there are traditional conventions about how an object should be displayed, or how a picture should be hung, but by playing games with design and turning things around, by looking at the way other cultures do things, refreshing new ideas can emerge.

East-West style also offers a new look at the way rooms are used. For those who live in crowded cities – from New York and London to Tokyo – space is at a premium in today's homes. The twentieth century has created so much more to fit into an ever-decreasing space. The answer lies in making fewer things work harder, doubling up their use, moving the same items from room to room. Traditional Japanese interiors re-semble an almost empty box in which the juniper crossbeams and latticework of walls and doors make a geometric pattern with no other distractions. Flexible, adaptable, open space is one of the most precious elements of the Japanese home and the impression

INSPIRATIONS

EVEN THE GLITTERING ROOFS OF BURMESE TEMPLES ARE A SOURCE OF INSPIRATION FOR HOPPEN. HERE SHE ECHOES THE EFFECT IN THE METALLIC FINISHES ON THE WOODWORK OF THE DOOR AND THE BED UPRIGHTS. SIMILARLY, THE PRINCIPLE OF USING ONE STRIKING JEWEL SHADE (THE PURPLE SOFA) IN A PREDOMINANTLY NEUTRAL BACKGROUND IS A VERY JAPANESE USE OF COLOUR. HER LOVE OF GEOMETRIC PRECISION, SEEN IN THE BROAD BORDERS OF THE BEDSPREAD AND THE ARRANGEMENT OF OBJECTS, LINKS ORIENTAL WITH OCCIDENTAL.

of spaciousness, in even a small apartment, generates energy and surprise. Screens are used as gentle delineators of space, often acting as the interface between inside and outside. Interconnecting rooms that flow easily from one to another ensure that spaces are never static. Flexibility is the key.

Rooms also have time-honoured roles. In Japan, for example, bathing is an ancient tradition, and the bathroom assumes an important status – more so than the bedroom, which in many homes barely exists. Where the bedroom often takes priority in a Western context, in Japan the bathroom is usually larger in relationship to the house than its Western counterpart, which may have been tacked on to the end of the house, carved out of bigger rooms or fitted into spare corners. You may not be able to change the architecture of your house, but you can give a room an oriental sense of importance in a Western way by using fine materials in what might otherwise be considered a mundane context.

The way a home is laid out, and the implications this may have for the future, is a fundamental concern that is common throughout much of China, embodied in the practice of *feng shui*, or the art of living in harmony with your environment. A broadly based body of principles, it promises prosperity and abundance, peace and serenity, health and longevity to those who fashion their homes according to its guidelines. And this underlying sense of order and simplicity, with everything placed strategically and for a purpose, is central to the East-West decorating philosophy, a meeting point for spirit, tradition and style.

INSPIRATIONS

COLOUR AND CONTRAST

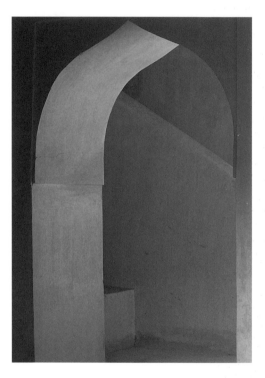

THE NATURAL COLOURS OF CREAM, EARTH AND STONE ALLOW THE EYE TO ENJOY ARCHITECTURAL DETAILS AND OUTLINES. THIS EFFECT IS SHOWN DRAMATICALLY IN AN OCHRE-COLOURED, ARCHED DOORWAY IN OMAN (BELOW).

People respond to colour instinctively, yet all too often such instincts are muffled when it comes to choosing colour in their own homes. East-West style is at times colourful and at others restrained, adapting colour techniques and customs from around the world to create stunning interiors. It is based on a philosophy drawn from cultures where the use of colour is naturally confident and rarely complicated. To understand the difference between a Western and Eastern use of colour, it is worth reflecting on artistic traditions. In Western art, paint colours tend to be mixed with each other to produce an infinite variety of tones and shades, and the first sketch will often be reworked before the final canvas is completed, whereas in the East pigments are always used in their original, clear state and the first brushstrokes are also the last.

THE ARCH MOTIF IS TAKEN UP IN THE GLAZED CUPBOARD DOORS OF A KITCHEN (LEFT), IN WHICH HOPPEN USES A NATURAL COLOUR THEME TO MINIMIZE ANY SENSE OF CLUTTER. IN A BEDROOM (OPPOSITE), TWO CARVED PILLARS AND A CREAM CURTAIN (USED AS A ROOM DIVIDER) CONVEY AN IMPRESSION OF FOUR-POSTER LUXURY WITHOUT ANY SENSE OF THE HEAVINESS THAT USUALLY ACCOMPANIES SUCH AN IMPOSING PIECE OF FURNITURE.

COLOUR AND CONTRAST

Where Western art is often complex, that from the East is distinguished by its strong graphic qualities. Both are equally valid and have much to offer each other.

The key to an oriental use of colour is to create a background of calm simplicity and then to add contrast, either with brilliant exclamations of colour or, more subtly, by introducing texture. These contrasts can shout dramatically or barely speak above a whisper – a quite different approach to traditional Western decorating styles whose charm often comes from the blending of tones and patterns, whether in the classic English country-house style, or the more stripped-down Scandinavian or French country interiors. As you go East there is increasing emphasis on the way the natural tones and textures work together without adornment: wood, bamboo, stone and wicker. In the Japan of today minimalist structures of concrete and steel may have replaced cedarwood beams and rice-paper panels, but the sense of geometrical order and respect for natural materials remains. Colour, although used less, becomes more of a statement, and is in many ways easier to enjoy. This doesn't mean giving up complex patterns and indulgent fabrics: an almost monochrome Eastern restraint is often the best backdrop for the most luxurious of Western fabrics and colours.

East-West style has essentially adapted a sparing use of colour from the monochrome traditions of Japan, often working within a spectrum that ranges from white and cream through all the natural shades of wood, clay, earth and stone, with all their myriad tones and textures. Black, often regarded as a non-colour and largely ignored in Western decorative schemes,

COLOUR AND CONTRAST

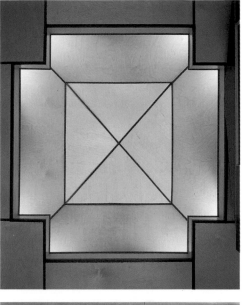

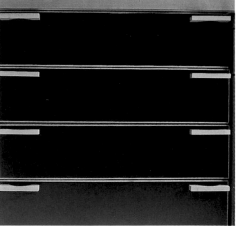

KELLY HOPPEN BORROWS THE USE OF BLACK, TO
OUTLINE AND DEFINE, FROM JAPANESE INTERIORS.
IN THIS KITCHEN SHE HAS USED BLACK LACQUER
AND MAPLE VENEER AS THE DOMINANT
MATERIALS. EVEN THE LIGHTING IS IN KEEPING
WITH THE STRICT GEOMETRY OF THE WHOLE.
CLEVERLY CONCEALED UPLIGHTERS IN EACH
CORNER OF THE CRUCIFORM CEILING CREATE
THE OPTICAL ILLUSION OF A SKYLIGHT.

BLUE AND YELLOW COME AT OPPOSITE ENDS OF THE COLOUR SPECTRUM AND THIS JAPANESE BEDROOM AND SILK WALL HANGING SHOW HOW EFFECTIVE IT CAN BE WHEN OPPOSITES ARE USED AS BACKGROUND AND HIGHLIGHT, RATHER THAN IN EQUAL QUANTITIES. BOTH THE SILK HANGING AND THE BEDROOM ARE PREDOMINANTLY DARK BLUE, WHILST THE LAMPSHADE AND THE SMALL SQUARE OF GOLD IN THE HANGING ALLUDE TO THE MOON IN A MIDNIGHT SKY. A GLASS JAR, ALMOST EXACTLY THE SAME SHADE OF BLUE, IS PLACED IN FRONT OF THE HANGING SO THAT THE GREEN LEAVES APPEAR ALL THE MORE VIVID, AND SEEM TO FLOAT IN THE AIR, LIKE AN ABSTRACT SCULPTURE.

is used to accentuate other colours, lending definition and form. Enjoyed as a colour in its own right in the East, it can be both vibrant and intense, providing a dramatic contrast – black lacquer against pale maple or a black frame against crisp white rice-paper.

Japan is renowned for its simple, understated use of colour. And it is the colour of indigo blue, above all, that still defines Japanese style today. It is used everywhere – on kimonos, on futons, on mats or *dojos*, on clothing worn everyday by farmers working in the fields, in fact on virtually any item made from cotton or raffia. As an inexpensive dye in a country that remained completely isolated from the outside world for two centuries, it was one of the few colours that was commonly available. Indigo leaves could be grown at home and then taken to the village to be used by the local dyer. It is also the only colour used in textile printing that will adhere to cloth without the need for complex mordanting procedures, and yet has good wash- and light-fast properties. These characteristics made it the most commonly used dye for clothing and textiles.

When contrasted with white, this becomes a colour scheme that works equally well in a Western context with Western fabrics: lengths of midnight-blue velvet can be suggestive of a medieval court as well as an imperial palace. Blue-and-white is also a typically Chinese colour theme, with oriental porcelain found in all the great interior styles of the world from the elegant yellow drawing rooms of John Fowler in Britain and Sister Parrish in the United States to the refreshingly pared-down interiors of Scandinavia. Its Western adaptation appears as charmingly naïve Dutch Delft tiles and willow-pattern crockery.

Equally, the use of colour in the East can be spectacularly brilliant: think of brightly painted Indian streets, the mosaics of Morocco, the sumptuous *yalis* or palaces along the Bosporus in Turkey, and the red lacquer peonies and dragons found painted on chests and masks from China to Tibet. India has its hot pinks, sunshine yellows and strident blues, yet even when these colours are found in plastics and other synthetic materials there is a lack of inhibition and a confidence about combining colour that is hard to equal in the West.

In India similar principles, interpreted differently, underlie an almost riotous use of colour. Sparse rooms make a perfect backdrop for brilliant colours. Even the most lavish Indian palaces were often simply painted white. And rather than the proliferation of furniture that you would expect to find in a comparable Western home, you might find just one piece of furniture – a heavily ornate and luxurious bed, perhaps made elaborate with gilded legs – and therefore a limited opportunity to use colour.

With so little clutter and such a plain background, a host of brilliant, dazzling colours can be indulged in, glorious bedhangings, in the vivid pinks and reds of women's saris, and even in the iridescent violets, pinks and electric blues which are often used to paint the outside of houses, creating bright blocks of colour that shimmer against their terracotta and ochre neighbours like a strip of glittering blue water against the sand. With over 300 natural plants to make dyes and a long tradition of understanding fixatives, the Indian love of colour is central to their culture. There is an instinctive understanding of tone and contrast – a coat of brilliant blue paint might be flung over a house, without bothering to prepare it or sand it down first, the blue then contrasting with pink or green windows and doors.

Colour delineates the caste system, entitling people to wear only a certain colour of turban. Each class has its distinguishing colour: white is the colour of priests, red is the colour of warriors, brown is the colour of merchants, saffron is the colour of sages and black denotes menial workers. Religious festivals, such as Diwali and Holi, are emphasized with colour – during Diwali houses are whitewashed and the wives of important men wear navy blue, while during Holi, everyone is drenched in coloured waters and dyes, so that you might see people in the streets coated in one shade of tangerine or cerise, literally from head to foot.

SAFFRON YELLOW, LIME GREEN AND IRIDESCENT PINK ARE THE COLOURS OF INDIA – VIBRANT AND PASSIONATE, AND BEST ENJOYED AGAINST NEUTRAL BACKGROUNDS. FLOWER PETALS ARE SOLD IN HESSIAN SACKS IN INDIAN MARKETS, AND HOPPEN TRANSLATES COLOURS AND CONTRASTS INTO AN INTERIOR SCHEME WITH TWO JEWEL-COLOURED ANTIQUE CHAIRS, PLACED AGAINST FINE OLD WOODEN CHESTS AND CREAM-COLOURED WALLS.

COLOUR AND CONTRAST

HUGE SWATHES OF PINK AND YELLOW PRINTED
COTTON FALL NATURALLY IN FOLDS IN A
TEXTILE FACTORY IN RAJASTHAN. BY USING THESE
VIBRANT COLOURS IN SOFT FURNISHINGS
HOPPEN IS ABLE TO ADD DRAMATIC HIGHLIGHTS
TO OTHERWISE NEUTRAL SCHEMES.

You can see variations on the same brilliant colours, depending on the local plants from which the dyes are made, all around the Pacific Rim countries – from the brilliant saris on the banks of the Ganges to the Gauguinesque pinks and greens of Polynesia. It is only recently that Westerners have adopted these vivid clashing blocks of colour, incorporating them into fashion cycles in contemporary homes. But once again, even when the impression is of a riot

of colour, the overall context is usually a simple one – plain blocks of indigo, magenta, orange or cyclamen are seldom combined with patterns that might distract and confuse the eye.

This appreciation of vibrant colour can be used in an East-West context as long as the various elements are kept simple and uncluttered, perhaps using brighter accent colours with plain backgrounds, creating a focus in a scheme that is otherwise based on a restrained palette. Strong colours in soft furnishings or upholstery fabrics can add a feeling of opulence,

THERE IS A WIDE RANGE OF TEXTURES TO BE FOUND IN EXOTIC HAND-WORKED FABRICS. BY USING RICHER SILKS, VELVETS AND BROCADES, AND DETAILS SUCH AS TASSELS, BUTTONING AND PIPING, KELLY HOPPEN CREATES A FEELING OF WARMTH.

COLOUR AND CONTRAST

whilst giving a room an uplifting sense of light and warmth. Colours can complement, or contrast with, the tones of natural materials. For example, the burnished red of lacquered wood can be echoed in the red tones of a fabric or the gilt detail of a mirror can be picked up in a vibrant yellow brocade.

Lacquer red is a classic contrast colour. Strong and striking, it instantly attracts attention. Red dyes have traditionally been costly in all cultures – it is difficult to abstract a good red colour from plantstuffs, many of the reds tending to verge on brown – and have therefore come to denote luxury and wealth, whether in medieval Britain or modern-day China. It is such a strong colour that it is generally used as a highlight – a few red berries on a scroll painting or in the detail of an ornate lacquer cabinet. The warmth that red can bring to a room may be achieved with one or two small red ornaments, such as an arrangement of dark red lacquered bowls or a lacquer-red tray – flashes of colour

RED IS OFTEN CONSIDERED TOO STRONG TO BE USED IN LARGE BLOCKS, BUT THE VERY STRENGTH OF THE COLOUR CAN BE AN ASSET EVEN IN SMALL QUANTITIES, BRINGING A TOUCH OF EXTRAVAGANCE. HOPPEN BORROWS THE COLOURS OF AN ORIENTAL CABINET (PREVIOUS PAGE) AND USES TEXTURE TO MAKE A RED DAMASK SOFA LOOK WARM AND WELCOMING RATHER THAN SLICK AND INTIMIDATING. THE RED OF THE SOFA AND CURTAINS COMBINE WITH THE ZEBRA PRINT TO CREATE A VISUALLY STRIKING WHOLE.

that can bring a room to life. Or be bold and introduce red as the principal focus with an eye-catching sofa. Teamed with black as an anchor colour, red can look vibrant without becoming overbearing.

East meets West decorating does not only mean using Eastern colours in a Western context, however. It can also mean using Western colours, such as a sharp citrussy lime green, in an Eastern way. It is a decorating philosophy that can easily be adapted in any home and used Eastern-style in blocks of a single shade, as a principal contrast to an otherwise neutral palette. Coir matting and calico walls, warmer than stark white, are the ideal starting point, creating a tranquil background for texture and shape. The same effect can be achieved with deep blue and silver against cream and white.

Such simplicity is at the core of an East-West use of colour. Instilling a sense of discipline means using just three or four different colours in a room. Such colours will usually be closely related to each other, perhaps even following on from each other in the colour spectrum, each a logical continuation of the one before, often barely more than a deeper or richer shade. Even natural shades have an underlying hint of colour, and this is why a shade that works well in one room can look muddy and dull in another. All colours run in a spectrum from hot to cold, with the warm end of the spectrum delineating the reds, yellows and oranges while the cool end covers the greens and blues. Shades of cream, beige or brown echo these tones, which is why you will find a beige with pink undertones, or a grey with blue ones. A 'warm' golden cream can look dull beside, say, a lime-green curtain from the cool end of the spectrum. However, a cream with a sharp hint of lemon, which would look almost fluorescent

COLOUR AND CONTRAST

in a 'warm' colour scheme of reds, will sit perfectly with lime green. Hang a length of lining paper, painted with your chosen colour, in your room for several days to see how neutrals and naturals work on your walls and with your lighting. Then introduce a highlight colour such as gold, or black to define shape and form, or a splash of Chinese red.

Colour, or the lack of it, informs our lives in almost every aspect, and the colours that we choose in terms of our clothes, or the interiors of our houses, make statements about us and the life-styles that we lead. Colour is an essential ingredient in any interior and should be given careful consideration; after all, the shades that you choose will go a long way in determining the mood or atmosphere in a room, thus giving a home a sense of calm or vibrancy, coolness or warmth. In a Western-style interior, colour is often sacrificed in favour of pattern. Approaching colour in a more Eastern way means developing a more discriminating attitude to the colours that you use, not only in terms of the colour of your walls but also the objects and furnishings that you choose to incorporate.

THE SIGHT OF A RED TURBAN AGAINST A BATTERED DOOR MAY BE NO MORE THAN A MEMORABLE GLIMPSE OF A MORE TRANQUIL WAY OF LIFE, BUT SUCH BRIEF VISIONS OFTEN LINGER, AND CAN TEACH YOU MORE ABOUT COLOUR AND CONTRAST THAN READING PAGES OF THEORY. HERE HOPPEN SHOWS HOW TO RECREATE SUCH INSPIRATIONAL IDEAS IN DECORATIVE TERMS WITH A SINGLE RUBY VELVET CUSHION GLOWING IN AN AIRY BEDROOM. SHE ALSO UTILIZES THE EFFECTS OF CONTRAST IN HER CHOICE OF MATERIALS – THE BED HANGINGS ARE MADE OF SHEER DAMASK AND THE BED LINEN IS FRESH WHITE COTTON, PROVIDING A STRIKING COUNTERPOINT TO THE RICHNESS OF THE VELVET CUSHION. DISTRESSED PAINT EFFECTS ON THE FURNITURE SOFTEN THE ALMOST MONASTIC AUSTERITY OF THE ROOM.

TEXTURE AND SURFACE

Just as the early trade routes opened the doors to new influences and cultures, so travel can open our eyes, providing an infinite source of inspiration. It can stimulate not only thoughts about why and where you use particular colours in your home, but also a new use of materials. The Italians, long known for their love of design, are particularly adept at turning an expensive item of furniture into something truly original by treating it casually – a gilded chair from a palazzo might be upholstered in cream calico. The contrast is dynamic and works well in either traditional or contemporary interiors. Nothing is too mundane, everything has a value – it only needs to be seen with different eyes.

Fabrics in themselves can be a source of inspiration: linen, velvet, Scottish tartan, raw silk, weaves and piqué can all be employed in unusual adaptations. Similarly, less obvious fabrics such as men's suiting, lining fabric, upholstery scrim and even carpet binding can be used to grace ottomans, armchairs and dining tables, or to edge cushions and bolsters. Learning how to use fabrics creatively, however costly or cheap, plays a major part in East-West style.

AN AERIAL VIEW OF A RICE FIELD IN NEPAL SHOWS THE PATTERNS MADE BY NATURE IN AN APPARENTLY HOMOGENOUS LANDSCAPE. THE WAY THE DIFFERENT FIELDS INTERSECT, THEIR COLOUR AND THE FURROWS OF CULTIVATION ALL OFFER INSPIRATION WHEN CHOOSING MATERIALS FOR THE HOME. HOPPEN DRAWS ON SUCH IMAGES WHEN GROUPING DIFFERENT TEXTURES TOGETHER – CHENILLE AND DEVORÉ VELVET LIE SIDE-BY-SIDE WITH HUMBLER HESSIAN. SIMILARLY, CREWELWORK CURTAINS ARE COMPLEMENTED BY THE ORNATENESS OF A CARVED TABLE, WHILE A VASE OF FLOWERS ECHOES THE FLORAL DESIGN OF THE INDIAN CREWELWORK.

TEXTURE AND SURFACE

In oriental cultures nothing is wasted, and an economy of style – using materials that may be expensive or cheap, traditional or contemporary, in innovative ways – is the key to this look. Metallic surfaces are borrowed from the gilded roofs of Burmese pagodas and transformed into decorative effects on woodwork inside the home, and the weave of the Japanese *tatami* mat is echoed in sisal and seagrass carpets. The way you use materials, whether they are traditional or the result of new technology, plays a leading role: a woven oriental fabric, for example, might be manufactured in more muted colours or a self pattern, giving ancient craftsmanship a new lease of life by making it clean and contemporary.

Pattern is a very distinctive way of calling attention to a fabric: nothing delineates a traditional English drawing-room so clearly as its rose-patterned chintz or a French country tablecloth as its naive Provençal print. However, in a style where cultures meet, pattern can make too obvious a statement, or it can be too restricting. If you want to keep your environment fluid and flexible, a floral-patterned curtain can limit your possibilities. And if you want to take the traditions of a culture and use them in a contemporary way, some patterns may look too much of a visual cliché to work successfully. But others

CLASSIC DESIGNS SUCH AS FLORALS, SEEN IN THIS CHINOISERIE SILK (ABOVE), HAVE A PLACE IN EAST-WEST STYLE. HOWEVER, WHILE SOME DECORATING TRADITIONS HEAP PATTERN ON PATTERN, HOPPEN ADOPTS THE EASTERN PHILOSOPHY OF RESTRAINT, AND RARELY USES MORE THAN ONE DOMINANT PATTERN IN A ROOM, SUCH AS THIS MATCHING TABLECLOTH AND CHAIR. SHAPE ALSO CONTRIBUTES TO THE 'PATTERNS' IN A ROOM. FOR EXAMPLE, PREDOMINANTLY CURVED SHAPES MAY BE OFFSET BY THE STRAIGHT LINE OF A LAMP (CENTRE), WHILE A TABLEAU OF BOXY OUTLINES IS SOFTENED BY THE CURVES OF A MIRROR FRAME AND A LARGE SPHERICAL BALL (FAR LEFT).

have become classics and have passed into the international lexicon of design, often those that have crossed from East to West and back again generations ago. Paisley, originally an Indian print based on the shape of a mango, is a recurrent theme in Western decorative styles, and has been picked up by American decorators such as Ralph Lauren and incorporated into a house style. A delicate floral-patterned silk in chinoiserie style can come into its own in an East-West scheme to create an oriental atmosphere. Other motifs, such as stripes, are open to numerous interpretations: strictly monochrome in black, white and brown on Japanese *dojo* mats, they reappear in a riot of reds, pinks and golds in a Persian palace; stripes can grow ornate in Venetian candy-twists, assume a restrained yet rich look in deep navy or burgundy redolent of the Regency or Napoleonic era, and look fresh in red-and-white cotton in a Long Island beach house. Checks, too, are international, the breezy innocence of Swedish or English country checks given more body when reinterpreted in Scottish tartan, or adapted to the East meets West

THE EAST MEETS WEST LOOK CAN BE RICHLY EMBROIDERED AND COLOURFUL AS WELL AS SIMPLE AND AUSTERE. HERE A ROW OF SCARLET-AND-PINK EMBROIDERED SLIPPERS FROM INDIA ARE HOPPEN'S INSPIRATION FOR A LIVING ROOM TREATMENT BASED ON CHINESE RED AND BLACK. DAMASK AND VELVET FABRICS ARE USED FOR THE CUSHIONS AND UPHOLSTERY, WHILE THE RAISED PATTERN OF SILK/VELVET STRIPES ON THE SOFA MAKE A DRAMATIC TEXTURAL CONTRAST TO THE GLEAMING WOODEN BOXES. THE WHOLE SCHEME IS RUTHLESSLY GOVERNED: SHE USES JUST TWO COLOURS (RED AND BLACK), TWO SHAPES (ROUND AND SQUARE) AND TWO PATTERNS (FLORAL AND STRIPE), SO THE EFFECT IS OPULENT WITHOUT BEING OVER-THE-TOP. IT IS A USEFUL DISCIPLINE TO REMEMBER WHEN WORKING WITH RICH MATERIALS AND STRONG COLOURS.

TEXTURE AND SURFACE

WHEN WALKING ON THE BEACH, ALONGSIDE A
MOUNTAIN STREAM, OR EVEN EXPLORING AN OLD
CHURCHYARD, NOTE THE TEXTURES AND
CONTRASTS PROVIDED BY NATURE. THE GREENS
AND BLACKS OF LICHEN OVER ROCK SUGGEST
COLOUR COMBINATIONS THAT HOPPEN
RECREATES IN VELVET AND HESSIAN. THE PROCESS
OF CHANGE AND WEAR GIVES ELEMENTS SUCH AS
WOOD AND STONE A DEPTH AND BEAUTY THAT
MAN-MADE OBJECTS CAN NEVER ACHIEVE – THINK
OF DRIFTWOOD, THE WEATHERBEATEN TILES OF
OLD ROOFTOPS OR THE FADED BUT ORNATE
WRITING OF AN OLD SHOP SIGN.

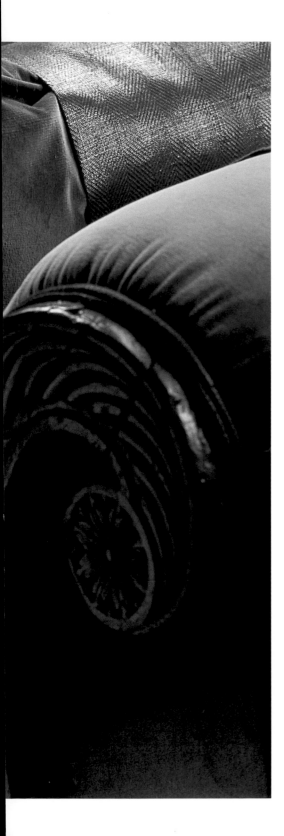

look by means of tapes or bindings sewn onto velvet in a giant criss-cross design. Embroidery, tapestry and crewelwork all have connotations of craftsmanship while animal prints have a defined personality all their own.

One of the most important decorative elements in Eastern pattern-making is calligraphy. Literally 'beautiful writing', calligraphy goes beyond mere communication. It is an art form in itself, and there is as much emphasis on beauty, style and composition as in any other form of painting. Fine paper, parchment and silk are graphically inscribed with pen, brush and ink and the tools of the calligrapher were status symbols enjoying great prestige as a manifestation of the intellect. In Western and Islamic societies, calligraphy was essentially a craft – used in the service of God, government or the aristocracy of the day. Only in the East is a calligrapher historically an artist in his or her own right, which may be why Chinese and Japanese scrolls are so decorative and elegant.

Many of the designs that feature in oriental textiles, or in silk carpets and rugs, depict the natural world – animals, insects and birds – in a highly stylized and graphic form. All have their own associations: the dragon represents imperial power, the peacock beauty, the cypress tree immortality, while the sacred lotus, perhaps one of the most evocative of Eastern images, symbolizes a great lineage. Just as different designs and motifs have their own associations, different types of fabric have their own characteristics: the lustre of Shantung

silk evokes the exoticism of China, the elaborate needlework of a *shashiko*-style jacket the mystery of Japan, whereas wool or velvet signal warmth and opulence in a Western context.

The drape of a fabric is another means of creating interest and making a statement with texture. The nineteenth-century Venetian designer, Mariano Fortuny, caused a sensation when he pleated silk, resulting in an effect that was quite different from flat material. Layering can be used to create an extra dimension on upholstery, juxtaposing colours, patterns or textures in a disciplined way. Layered effects add interest to furniture with box upon box, at windows where two qualities of fabric are shown off one against the other, even in the neat folds of a beautifully made bed, or in banners of fabric hanging down walls. Layers of fabric criss-crossing each other add an accent to a plain tablecloth, and a chaise longue becomes a still-life with a black sash folded *obi*-like down the centre and over the cushions.

An innovative use of materials is part of Eastern philosophy, which places the same importance on the craftsmanship in a wooden bowl as on a fine piece of furniture with ornate carving. Economy of line – beautiful clean shapes and colours – is reflected in an economical use of whatever comes to hand, and this works well in interiors as it allows you to throw off preconceptions about what works where, and to approach every room with an open mind. Once you have seen how effective the weave of upholstery scrim can look, used as a runner across a velvet tablecloth, or criss-crossing a silk cushion as a binding, you are freed from the fixed notion that only certain items or materials are right for certain rooms.

IN A SMALL HOUSE HOPPEN KEEPS THE LOOK LIGHT AND AIRY BY USING HARD MATERIALS, SUCH AS GLASS AND IRON, WHICH PROVIDE STRUCTURE BUT DO NOT IMPOSE ON A SMALL SPACE AS HEAVY WOODEN FURNITURE MIGHT. THE TRANSPARENCY OF THE GLASS ALLOWS THE LIGHT TO PASS THROUGH THE TABLETOP AND SHELF, OPENING UP ALL CORNERS OF THE ROOM. IT IS A VERY MONOCHROME, GRAPHIC LOOK WITHOUT FRILLS OR FUSS, BUT THE INTRODUCTION OF A NATURAL MATERIAL IN THE WICKER SEAT SOFTENS THE SCENE. NOTE HOW THE HERRINGBONE PATTERN OF THE WICKER ECHOES THE JAPANESE *TATAMI* FLOOR MAT AND THE LINES OF A FISHING BOAT. WOVEN WICKER IS A RECURRENT THEME THROUGHOUT BOTH THE EAST AND WEST, AND THE WARM HONEY TONES OF BASKETS AND MATS CAN PREVENT THE MOST MINIMALIST ROOM FROM LOOKING COLD OR BARE.

TEXTURE AND SURFACE

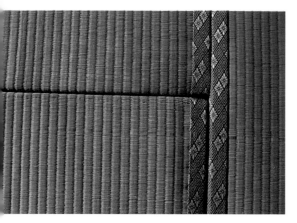

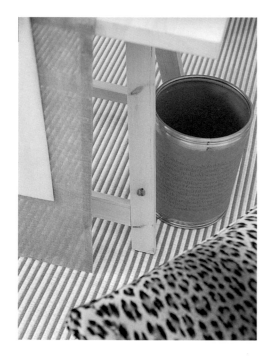

LEOPARD PRINT IS AN INTERIOR DESIGN CLASSIC
AND HERE HOPPEN SHOWS HOW IT CAN
LOOK OPULENT AND EXTRAVAGANT (RIGHT)
WHEN COMBINED WITH MARBLE, VELVET AND SILK
TASSELS, OR CLEAN AND CONTEMPORARY
AGAINST TAUPE-AND-WHITE STRIPES REMINISCENT
OF A JAPANESE *TATAMI* MAT (ABOVE AND TOP).

Texture can be so subtle that you hardly notice it as you move through a room. It provides depth, reflecting or absorbing light on surfaces, and preventing everything from looking 'flat'. Those who enter a traditional Japanese room for the first time have often been overwhelmed by the way in which a sparse simplicity brings textural detail alive: glowing polished wooden floorboards against a woven straw mat, the high gloss of a lacquer boxes against the rough wood of a trestle table made from old weathered planks. Such contrasts are pleasurable both to see and feel: luxurious fabric against everyday weaves, dark against light, soft against hard, natural against man-made.

Textural contrasts can be explored thematically too. Marble, granite, pebbles, slate and rock are all variations on stone, and have different textures and finishes that can draw the best out of each other. A group of sea-weathered pebbles on a polished marble surround in a bathroom highlights the distinction between stone that has been burnished by hand and that which has been smoothed and worked by the forces of nature. Slub, lustrous and embroidered silk reflect their individual qualities when seen against each other. Wood and wicker are both essentially the stems of trees, and have a grainy quality. Juxtaposing them displays the pliable, flexible nature of wicker against the strength and solidity of wood, while contrasting their similar hues. Iron and glass are both made from natural materials but have had their essential nature altered entirely by the manufacturing process. They partner each other in that they are both hard, smooth surfaces, yet they too have important differences.

You can also change the nature of a fabric by placing it in a different context. A leopard print cushion beside a monochrome *tatami* mat highlights its graphic qualities. The black-and-white stripes of the mat draw attention to the strong black outlines of the leopard spots. Yet the same leopard print fabric on a gilt stool beside a marble basin and a thick velvet curtain evokes a feeling of luxury and decadence. Leopard print, although a high fashion fabric, is in fact a natural classic – a pattern that works to great effect in a number of environments and styles. Other fabrics with similar qualities include leather, which can conjure up images either of travel or spartan modernism, depending on the context, and linen, which can be crisp and clean or a sign of opulence. All three are favourite fabrics in East-West style as they are flexible yet have defined personalities, are neutral yet never dull.

Walls can benefit from the textural approach. Of course, some walls have always been textured: oak panelling in medieval Europe, *shoji* screens in Japan, or the traditional *tadelakt* wall finish of Morocco, made of sand and quicklime, then polished to look like marble. Even

plain limewash, used the world over, has a softer, less even feel than brilliant white applied with a roller. Texture can be achieved in remarkably low-tech ways. For example, a speckled effect like that of old parchment can be created by covering paintwork that is still wet with newspaper. This is then brushed over, so that the newsprint adheres to the surface, and the paper is removed before the paint dries.

Flooring is kept simple and neutral in this decorative style. Bare boards, often polished to a warm glow, simple *tatami* mats and *dojos*, fitted sisal or coir carpeting, or natural-toned wool, plus the occasional warmth and flash of colour from a Turkish kilim or a contemporary rug. And where there is the occasional extravagance, such as a customized floor with inlays, texture can play its part: marble or slate with glass or wood. Natural textures provide the pattern, which keeps the whole look cool and under control.

The most exciting interiors are created when you look at materials, shapes and colours with a fresh eye, and use them in unexpected ways. Texture can be a creative tool in achieving this. Inexpensive materials can be treated in sophisticated ways: a chair covered in plain linen comes alive with cushions made of the most indulgent Fortuny silk or velvet, but you can also achieve stunning effects with scrim or hessian. A sofa need not be covered with a fussy chintz – its baroque lines may show up more beautifully with a simple upholstery cotton; conversely, a humble chair can be transformed with cushions made in a luxurious fabric.

The interplay between texture and surface is an important one in East meets West style and looking at walls and windows, floors and fabrics in new ways that incorporate elements of other cultural traditions provides an exciting design opportunity.

THE CONTRAST BETWEEN TWO TEXTURES NEED NOT BE EXTREME – HOPPEN JUXTAPOSES SIMILAR WEAVES IN A SERENE BEDROOM: SMOOTH COTTON LINEN AND A WARM FUR THROW AGAINST PLAIN WHITE WALLS MAKE A RESTRICTED SPACE LOOK LARGER. SIMILARLY, A HUMBLE CHEST OF UNVARNISHED PINE IS SET AGAINST BARE BOARDS, IN A WAY THAT EVOKES THE NATURAL SIMPLICITY OF ARCHITECTURAL DETAIL IN A TRADITIONAL JAPANESE HOUSE (RIGHT).

TEXTURE AND SURFACE

OBJECTS AND ACCENTS

BLUE AND WHITE IS ONE OF THE MOST POPULAR COLOUR SCHEMES IN CHINA AND JAPAN, AND IT HAS TRAVELLED WEST OVER THE CENTURIES TO BECOME A EUROPEAN CLASSIC, TOO. WHEN DISPLAYING CHINA, SYMMETRY AND REPETITION MAKE FOR MAXIMUM EFFECT: EIGHT BLUE-AND-WHITE CHINA CUPS ARE NEATLY PAIRED, AND THE OCCASIONAL UP-TURNED CUP PREVENTS THE DISPLAY FROM LOOKING STATIC. HOPPEN GROUPS THE THREE CHINESE JARS TOGETHER FOR A MORE INFORMAL DISPLAY, BUT THIS ARRANGEMENT IS HELD TOGETHER THROUGH SHAPE RATHER THAN SIZE. INFORMAL GROUPINGS LOOK BEST WITH ODD NUMBERS WHILE FORMAL ONES SHOULD BE EVEN.

The polished serenity of a carved Buddha, the translucency of gleaming blue oriental porcelain, the swirling generosity of a smooth wooden bowl and the ornate carvings of a Venetian mirror – these are the elements that turn a pleasing room into an inspired interior. Possessions are the passport to the personality of a room's owner, and paintings, statues, china, glass and objets d'art each tell their own story – of romance, travel or perhaps some distant childhood memory. It is through arranging and displaying these possessions that Eastern principles can work with Western artefacts, and objects from all over the world can be viewed together as a harmonious whole.

In countries where Buddhism has been the major religion for thousands of years, there is a long tradition of fine craftsmanship that begins in the humblest villages and reaches its peak in elaborate temples, the ultimate expression of a faith that sees the skill of a craftsman as a sacred gift. Statues for worship were made from the most basic materials, such as straw, terracotta or cow dung, by those who had great faith but little formal training. In Japan the Shinto religion follows similar lines. Essentially an animistic belief, Shintoism proposes that God is found in one's surroundings – an ancient tree, a stretch of water or a woodland pool may be considered sacred, and shrines are set up at the roadside to honour these places. By effectively acting as an interface between the sacred and material world, the craftsmanship

in even the most mundane utensils is valued. The tools and skill of the craftsman are honoured in a similar way, and the creative process is viewed as a spiritual act. Such ideals – and the results, with all their charming imperfections – are refreshing to the Western eye jaded by mass-production. The result is that even household objects can be seen as things of beauty.

A combination of simple design and ornate craftsmanship in an interior works best when seen in the context of an Eastern sense of balance. This can be seen visually: in old and new, in modern and antique, or in a combination of informal and precious artefacts. Most obviously seen in a set of objects arrayed in a grid system, or in rows as collections of twos, threes and fours, this love of structure and order does not require everything to be the same, simply that it should be balanced. As well as through the more regimental marshalling of forms, balance is achieved through the concepts of *yin* and *yang*, the essential forces of nature that are necessary counterweights to each other. For a room to be harmonious, both must be present. *Yin*, amongst other qualities, stands for dark colours, curves and wandering lines, and receptiveness, while *yang* is light, white, straight and linear. These principles are at their most effective when used to pull together the disparate objects that fill every home, when counterbalance and repetition are used to make visual sense of what would otherwise be merely clutter. These principles of

harmony and order can be adapted to incorporate the opulence and detailed workmanship of the West and the spirituality and simplicity of the East – the *yin* and the *yang* of two different cultures – in order to achieve a balance that is right for your home.

Everyone is familiar with the concept of a focal point in a room – and in Western homes this is usually the mantelpiece, the windows or a stunning painting. The focal point in an Eastern home was traditionally the hearth (known as the *irori* in Japan), which was situated in the centre of the main living area. Other focal points were, and still are, the household altars which were essentially elaborate still-life compositions, decorated with the greatest care and attention. The East-West style adopts the oriental love of grouping and order to create several minor focal points.

Each corner, alcove or set of furniture offers an opportunity for creating a small still-life composition. The word 'still-life' is perhaps misleading, as one of the keys to this decorating style is that it is essentially fluid. A group of Thai pots may be a tablescape one week and a mantelscape the next. This is a very Japanese attitude: the *tokonoma*, or display alcove, may contain at any one time a beautifully painted scroll, a statue and a flower arrangement, each carefully chosen to work together to reflect a season, a celebration or

THE GEOMETRIC LINES OF THE PADDY FIELDS AND THE CIRCULAR COOLIE HATS OF THE RICE-PLANTERS (PREVIOUS PAGE) STRIKE AN UNUSUAL ECHO IN THESE WIRE SHELVES HUNG WITH HATS. THE JUDICIOUS USE OF ASYMMETRY IS THE KEY TO THIS DISPLAY – HOPPEN HANGS TWO HATS ON THE RIGHT, ONE ON THE LEFT, WHILE A SQUARE PICTURE BALANCES THE MANY CIRCULAR SHAPES OF THE BOWLS. OTHER SHAPES INSPIRED BY TRAVEL, LIKE THIS LAVISH ARCH (ABOVE) IN AN INDIAN ROYAL PALACE, ARE SUGGESTED IN THE USE OF ELABORATE FRAMES. A HUGE, ORNATE MIRROR MAKES A FORMAL STILL-LIFE OF A GAP BETWEEN TWO CURTAINS; FOR A MORE INFORMAL EFFECT, HOPPEN PLACES A GILT-FRAMED PAINTING CASUALLY ON A MEZZANINE FLOOR.

THE STYLIZED GEOMETRIC PATTERNS DEPICTED ON
ALL FORMS OF DECORATIVE ART FROM DOORWAYS
TO KILIMS HAVE BECOME A COMPLEX DECORATIVE
TRADITION IN ISLAMIC COUNTRIES WHERE THE
DEPICTION OF LIVING CREATURES IS FORBIDDEN.

an honoured guest. Scrolls and statues not on display are neatly put away behind sliding doors – a complete contrast to the Western need to display all, or most of, your ornaments at once. A major part of arranging ornaments is editing them – learning not only what can be added to an arrangement but also what can be taken away.

Colour, form and proportion are all important aspects to consider when grouping objects for display. A corner, the end of a corridor, a set of shelves – all these offer opportunities for small set pieces. First, ask yourself what you would like to achieve with the display. Sometimes everything in a room is too evenly matched or toned, and you need something to act as an accent or highlight. Perhaps your room is a symphony of cream and white, or several shades of honey blended together in harmony. A dramatic splash of red, perhaps in a neat pile of Chinese lacquered boxes in ascending sizes, will give a corner impact. Or you may have a simple, blank wall which would be the perfect canvas for the sculptural outline of a distinctive silhouette – a glossily serene Buddha, a curvaceous terracotta pot or a bronze sculpture will all add interest and elegance. Think about what you might expect of each arrangement, and try out the opposite. A narrow piece of wall between two curtains looks like the ideal spot for a small painting, but try a large ornate mirror in the space and see whether a different approach works. Often it does, to stunning effect.

A sense of shape is a key element when grouping objects for display, encouraging a subconscious association between otherwise disparate objects. Simple overriding shapes like straight lines or curves serve as an antidote to highly decorative objects, and the more ornate and colourful Eastern and Western designs can thus be pulled together. This ensures that exotic decorative features – a riot of dragons or peonies – do not look out of place in an East-West setting; rather they bring the skills and traditions of the past in line with contemporary interiors. If you want an organic natural shape, go for odd numbers – three stone balls, five lacquered boxes or seven calligraphy brushes. If you want a more disciplined look, arrange objects according to even numbers. Look for points of unity to pull groups together – circular and cylindrical shapes, a certain colour such as purple or mauve, or a texture, such as the shine of brass or the veining of tortoiseshell, marble or slate.

Displaying collections is an art in its own right, and this is where Eastern style can be particularly inspirational. If you walk through a market in Thailand or Japan, you will see that even a tray of radishes, or a shop window full of knives, is beautifully displayed. Disciplined

STYLIZED PATTERNS DOMINATE THIS LIVING ROOM FROM THE PAISLEY PATTERNED CHAIR AND TURKISH KILIM TO THE CARVED STONE FIRE-SURROUND, THE ROUGH AFRICAN ARTEFACTS AND THE ORNATELY CARVED INDIAN TABLE.

OBJECTS AND ACCENTS

rows make the most of shape and colour, and extra touches – a red or purple tie around the vegetables, or an intricate knot – add highlights. Objects as well as food are presented with careful attention to detail to produce a visually balanced whole. Collections do not need to be valuable as even the humblest objects have a new sense of importance when shown together in a group. Forming a collection is an excellent way of enjoying your possessions, as most owners find that they become interested in the history and use of each object and gain a new understanding of their possessions and how they work together.

It is always effective to display a collection on shelves, uninterrupted by other details and allowing the main characteristic of each item to speak for itself. When there is a great deal of variety within the collection – antique glass, for example, may be Venetian, Georgian and Egyptian and in twenty or thirty different colours – then a simple treatment usually works best. Alternatively, you can adopt the Japanese stepped system for displaying objects. Shelves that go part of the way across a wall space in variable lengths are devised in what the Japanese call the *chigai-dana* or 'broken mist' manner, and this creates more air around the collection than would be achieved by rows of shelves running from wall to wall. There is also the traditional Japanese chest, called a *kaidan-dansu*, which would normally fit under a staircase, following its lines. Now often left free standing, its regular stepped surfaces make a perfect platform for display. Shelves can be chosen to complement or contrast with a collection – a set of Provençal baker's shelves or a Regency bookcase would both be as good a display case for a collection of Chinese or Thai celadon ware as a contemporary Japanese-designed set of shelves.

Flexibility is one of the most important aspects of the East-West style. Essentially a state of mind, it should extend to all decorative elements from the positioning of furniture to the placement of art and objects. With this in mind, there is probably more discussion about the correct way to hang pictures than any other area of display. The East-West style eschews the predictable routine of spacing pictures out evenly and using every wall. Free-up your walls and create a sense of movement by looking at them differently. Pictures can be arranged to form symmetrical or asymmetrical compositions of their own. A set of reproduction prints can look as effective as an Old Master drawing, and a child's painting as appropriate as an impressive work in oil. The first question to ask, however, is whether the painting is an accent, or whether it is a focus for the room, and develop the theme from there. While the Chinese, like the Japanese, change their wall scrolls around

TWO POTS OF BULBS AND A HANGING (RIGHT) MAKE A COMPOSITION OUT OF STRAIGHT LINES, THE NARROW BUDS STANDING ERECT LIKE SENTRIES AGAINST THE BROAD STRIPES OF THE FABRIC. SYMMETRY AND ASYMMETRY ARE THE KEY TO HOPPEN'S DISPLAYS AS SEEN IN A COLLECTION OF CHINA JARS (ABOVE). THE PLACEMENT OF OBJECTS IS ESSENTIAL FOR AN EASTERN FEEL, AND EVEN STORAGE CAN BECOME PART OF THIS AESTHETIC. THE OPEN DOOR OF A CUPBOARD IN AN ORIENTAL SHOP DISPLAYS ITS WARES.

BOWLS ON A ROUND TABLE CREATE A DISPLAY WHICH IS ALMOST ENTIRELY BASED ON CIRCLES. HOPPEN ECHOES THE SHAPE OF THE TABLE IN THE THREE BOWLS, AS WELL AS IN THE VASE AND THE OPEN FLOWERS. THIS SHOWS HOW REPETITION – OF SIZE, SHAPE OR COLOUR – CAN WORK SUCCESSFULLY IN SMALL TABLE-SCAPES TO PREVENT A GROUP OF SEVERAL OBJECTS FROM LOOKING LIKE CLUTTER. THE ROUND BUTTONS AND NEUTRAL COLOUR OF THE ADJACENT FLOOR CUSHIONS TAKE UP THE THEME.

regularly, believing that looking at the same art all the time will make you stale, the Western inclination is to crowd all the walls with images. There is no right and wrong way to do things, but adopting an Eastern approach will encourage a more disciplined selection of items as well as make a room feel fresh and different. Once again, you can invoke the principles of contrast to create a striking effect – one wall may have the simplicity of a single scroll hanging, the other a group of traditional gilt-framed oils.

Another aspect of flexibility comes with the dual function of many decorative objects, which may have a practical bias as well. This is particularly relevant in today's crowded cities and towns, where the most effective use of space is to make storage a part of the decoration. Baskets are one of the world's oldest forms of storage, and boxes and baskets arranged in tiers or rows can replace the conventional cupboard. The renewed respect for handcrafted

OBJECTS AND ACCENTS

work and natural materials, as well as their flexibility and capacity to hold difficult shapes, makes them a popular storage choice and beautifully crafted baskets have a decorative quality all of their own. Basketwork can be rough and earthy, such as big sturdy log or linen baskets, or it can be elegantly varnished and delicately wrought, as in the exquisite lacquered lunch baskets and wedding baskets from China, Thailand and Burma. Small, flexible reed baskets are ideal for desktops or dressing tables, holding pens, brushes or lipsticks, while larger rectangular wicker baskets are perfect for everything from shoes to shopping.

In many Asiatic countries the art of placement has developed into a philosophy of its own. The way the home is set out and the arrangement of possessions are seen to have implications for the rest of one's life, affecting areas as diverse as personal relationships and financial prosperity. In particular, the philosophy of *feng shui* explores the nature of design and arrangement. It affirms that a house should be arranged according to the principles of simplicity and beauty, as well as those of design and function. Central to these precepts is the belief that energy must be allowed to flow freely through a house. Too many bits and pieces will make your mind as cluttered as your home, and clogged-up corners obstruct the flow of good fortune. This does not mean that interiors have to be bland, simply that each possession should be carefully considered and placed according to its purpose. However these principles are applied, whether literally or loosely, oriental sensibilities can change the way you look at a room, replacing chaos with a calm, streamlined sense of equilibrium.

SIMPLE SHAPES MAKE PLEASING COMPOSITIONS WHEN SET OUT IN AN ORDERLY WAY. THE CURVE OF THIS BRASS MOROCCAN VASE EMERGES THROUGH THE LATTICEWORK OF A TRADITIONAL SCREEN. HOPPEN TAKES UP THIS BRASS THEME IN THE DISPLAY OF A SET OF OPIUM WEIGHTS, PLACED NEATLY BESIDE A HAND-BEATEN DISH AND A BRASS LAMP. THE LACK OF AN EVEN NUMBER OF WEIGHTS DOES NOT WORRY HOPPEN. IN FACT, THE GAP IN THE BOTTOM RIGHT-HAND CORNER ENHANCES THE SQUARE OUTLINE OF THE ARRANGEMENT.

SIMPLICITY

AS A PHILOSOPHY OF LIFE, BUDDHISM HAS SPANNED
NEARLY FIVE THOUSAND YEARS OF PAN-ASIAN
CULTURE, AND IN EACH ARTISTIC REPRESENTATION
OF BUDDHA THE ARTIST STRIVES TO DISTIL THE
PRECEPTS OF SERENITY AND PEACE, WHICH ARE
AT THE HEART OF THE BUDDHIST FAITH. THE
MATERIAL USED IS OF THE UTMOST IMPORTANCE
AND BRONZE, WOOD OR STONE ARE THE MOST
COMMON. EACH OF THESE MEDIA GIVES A
DIFFERENT EFFECT, FROM THE DEEPLY INSCRUTABLE
DEPTHS OF EBONY TO THE RADIANCE THAT
EMANATES FROM A BRONZE STATUE. ULTIMATELY
IT IS THE CONVICTION AND FAITH OF THE
INSPIRED ARTIST THAT CONJURES UP THE TRUE
BEAUTY OF BUDDHA.

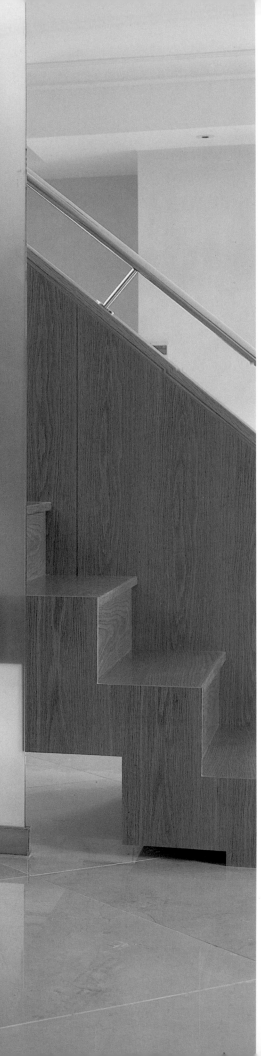

As our lives grow more complex, and the pressures and pace of modern life-styles become more demanding, simplicity is becoming an increasingly important issue. To an eye jaded by thousands of images during the day – through advertising, in shops and at work – the idea of returning to a home where all is calm and serene seems very alluring. Those who work in highly visual areas, such as designers and artists, place an especially high value on the enduring qualities of simplicity and this may go some way to explaining the new interest in minimalism in both the fashion and interior worlds. In both the West and the East, spirituality has traditionally been fostered in a plain, ordered environment, as if by shedding the worst excesses of materialism it is easier to develop an understanding of the issues in our lives that really matter.

There is another reason why simplicity is increasingly sought after. Today's crowded cities and spreading suburbs mean that space is now one of the most precious commodities, whether you live in the teeming capitals of Tokyo, Peking or Hong Kong, or the equally busy but often more spread-out conurbations that surround New York, London and Paris. Houses are being carved up into apartments, apartments into studios, and family houses are getting smaller every year. It is only in the conversion of large-scale industrial buildings, such as warehouses, office blocks and lofts, that compromises on room size or allocation can be avoided, and this is part of their ever-increasing appeal. Interior design is now no longer focused merely on decorative issues, but on the way you actually use and maximize your living space to create an atmosphere that *feels* airy and spacious, even if the room is not.

A growing awareness of visual pollution in an over-crowded world also leads to a desire for paring down. Visual pollution is more than a skyline blemished by factory chimneys or a litter-strewn street. A constant stream of advertorials runs through our lives round the clock: radio, television, billboards as well as new electronic media. This places great pressure on people to buy, to achieve, and to be something or someone that very often they cannot be. Calm, order and simplicity in a home environment can screen out some of this visual clutter, and restore a sense of self and serenity. Eastern philosophies of simplicity and paring down answer a very particular need in today's societies in which the possession-conscious attitude that was so prevalent in the Eighties is now being superseded by a concern for a better quality of life. An improvement in life-style and in the quality of free time is now a prime concern, and by paring down we are not only able to free-up space, but time as well.

SIMPLICITY

It is important to adapt these attitudes and decorating styles to your home rather than adopt them wholesale from other cultures. The variation in life-styles between countries places different demands and priorities on a home – the Japanese, for example, rarely entertain at home, preferring to do so in restaurants, keeping the home private and a family affair. It is the reverse in many North European or North American homes, where part of the pleasure of having a beautiful house is inviting friends and family to enjoy it, too. Similarly other cultures may place different levels of importance on the various rooms in a house – in the West the bedroom is a key room, whereas in the East the washroom will be given priority. Such considerations need to come first when borrowing ways of living from other countries, so that you can interpret, rather than impose, a style on your home.

SIMPLICITY

CONCENTRIC CIRCLES CONCENTRATE THE
MIND ON THE BEAUTY OF THE SIMPLEST SHAPES
AND FORMS. THIS CAN BE SEEN IN THE
NEATLY RAKED GRAVEL IN THE TOFUKU JI ZEN
GARDEN IN KYOTO – ONE OF THE MOST
TRADITIONAL CITIES TO BE FOUND IN JAPAN.
THE GLOBE, WITH ITS CONNOTATIONS OF THE
EARTH AND THE PLANETS, IS A POWERFUL
IMAGE. HOPPEN TAKES TWO GIANT MARBLE
SPHERES AND ANCHORS A MANTELPIECE BY
PLACING THEM AT ITS BASE. THEY REPLACE THE
MORE USUAL LOG BASKET AND FIRE IRONS WHICH
WOULD NOT, IN ANY CASE, BE APPROPRIATE
FOR MANY INNER-CITY FIREPLACES. HOPPEN TAKES
INTO CONSIDERATION THE LINE OF THE FIRE
SURROUND, WHICH IS ECHOED HERE IN THE
CIRCULAR SHAPE OF THE STONES. THE ESSENCE
OF THIS DISPLAY IS SIMPLICITY: A NEUTRAL
PALETTE, A SINGLE SHAPE AND ONE DOMINANT
MATERIAL – MARBLE – WHICH ALL COMBINE TO
GIVE A FEELING OF TRANQUILLITY.

THIS WROUGHT-IRON DETAIL (BELOW) IS TAKEN FROM AN OLD GATE IN ALGERIA AND SHOWS THE PATTERNS USED IN TRADITIONAL SAHARAN ARCHITECTURE. THE USE OF WROUGHT IRON IN FURNITURE IS GAINING POPULARITY – FORMERLY A RUSTIC MATERIAL, ITS STRENGTH AND FLEXIBILITY MAKE IT A GOOD CHOICE FOR MODERN, URBAN DESIGNS. HOPPEN USES IT IN SMALL ROOMS TO MAKE THE MOST OF SPACE AND TO GIVE AN AIRY FEEL TO LARGER ITEMS OF FURNITURE. HERE, ANGULAR BLACK OUTLINES MAKE A GRAPHIC CONTRAST TO WHITE WALLS, AND THE MONOCHROME THEME IS ECHOED IN THE WIRE BASKET AND SPHERICAL BALLS ON THE SIDE TABLE. WHEN TREATED IN A CONTEMPORARY WAY, IRON FURNITURE IS EXTREMELY FLEXIBLE, MOVING EASILY FROM ROOM TO ROOM AND FROM INSIDE TO OUTSIDE, SO THAT A GARDEN CHAIR CAN BE PULLED UP AT THE DINING TABLE OR CAN SIT JUST AS HAPPILY IN THE BATHROOM.

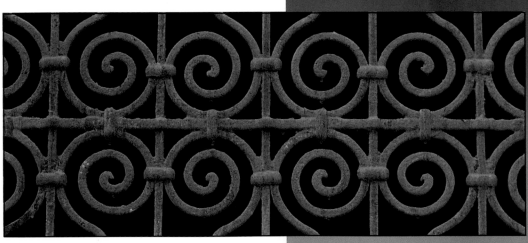

In densely populated countries like Japan, India and China people cannot afford the space for too many unnecessary possessions, so a simpler way of life has developed. Yet a Western life-style demands a certain number of objects and furnishings – because we sit on chairs, for example, rather than on cushions on the floor, we also require side tables beside them for lamps or places to leave books or drinks. Sometimes the answer is to be creative about finding new and multiple uses for your favourite things, borrowing the principles from the barely furnished households of the East. A vase may hold flowers one day, or be transferred to a desk for pens and brushes the next. Simplicity does not only mean clearing away clutter, but re-thinking the way you live. Free yourself of anything you do not really love or use. You may not wish to get rid of things that you

SIMPLICITY

A SERIES OF BUILT-IN CUPBOARDS IN A
JAPANESE INTERIOR AND THE TYPICAL DISPLAY
ALCOVE OR *TOKONOMA*, WITH ITS CHEQUERBOARD
BACKGROUND, USE THE FULL HEIGHT OF THE
ROOM IN A CITY WHERE SPACE IS PRECIOUS.
TO MAXIMIZE SPACE IN A STUDIO APARTMENT
(FAR RIGHT) HOPPEN CREATES A MEZZANINE
OVER THE DOOR. FOR DECORATION SHE
USES SIMPLE BANNERS MADE FROM CALICO AND
UPHOLSTERY SCRIM WHICH ECHO THE GRID
SYSTEMS SO COMMON IN JAPANESE HOUSES.
THESE GEOMETRIC LINES ARE REPEATED
IN THE FOREGROUND WITH A LINEN RUNNER
PLACED ALONG THE BLEACHED WOOD OF
THE TABLE – SUCH DECORATIVE ELEMENTS
ARE TYPICALLY JAPANESE IN STYLE.

have owned for many years, so borrow the oriental custom of keeping art and decorative objects tucked away, bringing them out when it is appropriate to certain occasions or times of year.

The move towards a more pared-down look is gathering momentum in the West, with minimalist architects such as Richard Rogers and John Pawson, as well as a range of shops and galleries, epitomizing an ideal of stylish, minimal living. Yet many people are still apprehensive of rooms where the main statement is made by just one or two objects, perhaps because it makes such a strong statement about their taste and style. Yet there is nothing to fear by making the most of the shape and colour of a piece of furniture or an object, rather than covering it with fabrics or cushions, or losing it in a crowd of miscellaneous bric-a-brac. It brings the quality of craftsmanship and materials to the fore – and shows off anything that is beautifully and lovingly made, or that means a great deal to you. With fewer objects and decorative features to distract the eye, the qualities of design and craftsmanship assume greater importance, and an integrity of their own that stands the test of close scrutiny. In Japanese homes the architecture itself sets high and exacting standards for the objects brought into it,

SIMPLICITY

and any inherent weakness is exposed when set in such a demanding context. Good design and fine craftsmanship should recognize the qualities inherent in each and every element, their strengths and how they can be used to best effect, whether fine porcelain or earthy terracotta.

This does not mean spending large sums of money. It means picking the elements in a room you really love and emphasizing them, clearing away things that are just there because there is nowhere else to put them. If your favourite picture is a simple line drawing of a child's face, or even a poster of a faraway place, give it space and prominence so that you can enjoy it. Do not feel that you have to hang 'important' art in the prime position. Feel free to listen to your own taste and values, and if you tire of the picture after a while, switch it around. Once again, this means throwing off preconceptions about which materials are 'best'. This decorating philosophy places as much importance on unpretentious scrims, cottons and calicos as on fine velvets and silks. Humbler materials may have imperfections, but they often have a warmth that goes beyond materialism and mass-manufacture.

Attention to detail is an important element in simplicity. The restrained, neatly methodical architecture of a Japanese interior, for example, with its straight lines, mono-chromatic colours and pared-down rooms, draws the eye to the architecture of the building itself. Yet the elaborate plaster cornicework on a Victorian ceiling can go virtually unnoticed, such is the distraction from the room below. A concentration on such details is the hallmark of craftsmanship throughout the East, not only when working on simple forms but also when creating fantastically elaborate ornaments or religious icons – from the intricate gold-worked glass and ornate tiling of Istanbul to the delicate calligraphy and richly-patterned porcelain of China. Such glorious workmanship may seem the opposite of simplicity, but if enjoyed against an uncluttered, tranquil background can act as a decorative counterpoint to the scheme as a whole.

The physical shortage of space is undoubtedly the greatest driving force in the increasing interest in East-West style. An uncluttered, controlled approach to space, colour, and the use of furniture can open out rooms. Repeating colours and shapes gives a sense of order and continuity to an interior, and creates an illusion of space flowing freely between rooms. A rich blue may be used on the bedroom curtains, emerge again in a living-room rug or on the trim of a tablecloth, be repeated in the china in the

TAKE TWO SITTING ROOMS: BOTH ARE BASED
AROUND WHITE WALLS, NEUTRAL FURNISHINGS
AND NATURAL FLOORING, AND YET ONE RETAINS
AN AIR OF FORMALITY, WHILST THE OTHER IS
RELAXED AND WELCOMING. A PROFUSION OF
WHITE CANDLES AND EXOTIC WHITE ORCHIDS
ADD SPARKLE AND SOFTNESS (PREVIOUS PAGE),
PERFUMING THE AIR AND GIVING THE ROOM A
WARM AND TRANQUIL GLOW. THE LARGE MIRROR
REFLECTS THE LIGHT FROM THE CANDLES AND
THE GEOMETRIC ARRANGEMENT OF THE PICTURES
ON THE OPPOSITE WALL, WHICH LENDS THE ROOM
A SENSE OF PERSPECTIVE THAT DRAWS YOU IN
TOWARDS THE WELCOMING FIREPLACE. IN
CONTRAST, A MORE FORMAL ATMOSPHERE CAN
BE RETAINED. THIS ROOM (RIGHT) TAKES ITS
DRAMATIC IMPACT FROM FOUR GIANT CANDLE-
STICKS RANGED ALONG THE MANTELPIECE. THESE
CANDLESTICKS WOULD USUALLY STAND ON
THE FLOOR, BUT THEIR HEIGHT BALANCES THE
HEIGHT OF THE FIREPLACE EXACTLY, AND HAVING
FOUR, RATHER THAN ONE AT EITHER END,
STRIKES A LESS CONVENTIONAL NOTE. THEY ALSO
SHOW HOW ONE OVER-THE-TOP ELEMENT IN A
ROOM LOOKS VERY EFFECTIVE AGAINST AN
OTHERWISE PLAIN BACKGROUND. THE ATMOSPHERE
CAN BE CHANGED IN MOMENTS BY SIMPLY
ADDING OR TAKING AWAY DIFFERENT ELEMENTS.
THE CHAIRS ARE VICTORIAN, AND WOULD
TRADITIONALLY BE UPHOLSTERED IN A PATTERN
OR DARK VELVETS, BUT PLAIN CREAM FABRIC
DRAWS ATTENTION TO THEIR DESIGN.

kitchen, and so on. A clever use of furniture can help, too. The Japanese have long had a tradition of dual-purpose furniture, with futons unrolled at night and replaced by cushions for seating during the day.

In other countries, such as Thailand, the concept of a separate bedroom is rare in traditional housing – in fact, only practical rooms, such as kitchens and bathrooms, have a specific designation. In a traditional oriental home the washroom symbolizes cleanliness, and washing has evolved into a highly ritualized procedure. Only the best materials are used and special windows are sometimes built-in to offer scenic views for the bather. The bath, or *ofuro*, is so valued in Japan that the size of the room is often considerably larger than the kitchen, the reasoning being that it is here, rather than anywhere else in the house, that a person frees themselves from the anxieties of the day. In contrast, most of the other rooms in the house are combined to form multi-purpose living spaces.

Rooms in Western homes, on the other hand, are usually designated specifically for one purpose, while the inside and the outside of the house are clearly separated. This automatically increases the amount of furniture needed, with kitchen chairs differentiated from more formal dining-room chairs, and so on. Freeing-up living space by giving it multiple functions is part of a simpler way of life. This does not mean discarding the furnishing traditions of the West, but looking at how you can make them work in different ways. Items that are decoratively neutral are far more flexible, and can be moved from room to room according to where they are needed rather than being rigidly allocated to one use and a specific room. A plain cream calico chair will sit elegantly in a dining room or comfortably in a bedroom. Simplicity, therefore, is not only about a disciplined approach to furnishings but about viewing space as flexible and interchangeable – dual-purpose rooms such as kitchens which do duty as dining rooms, bedrooms where people also relax and sit, and living rooms with a home office at one end, are all essentially 'living space' re-worked into different permutations. Although it may require a certain amount of discipline when adopting a new attitude to spatial arrange-ment and flexible furnishings, the final result will be a new sense of freedom.

Another Eastern tradition is the importance of the courtyard or garden and this is also an essential ingredient in simple living. The screens of Japanese houses can be removed to open up the entire structure to the outside elements, allowing nature to penetrate into the heart of the house. This inclusion of the natural world in the home has, in many cultures,

SIMPLICITY

been seen to offer a more peaceful and relaxing environment in which to live. Water is, of course, a major feature and the use of water to inspire a contemplative frame of mind can be seen in religions as diverse as Islam (for example, the beautiful waterways of the Alhambra) and Zen Buddhism, and historically, water has also been important in many Western traditions – Platonists believed that water, in reflecting light, reflected the soul. Many of these features are not feasible in a Western home, but ideas like the Japanese concepts of *sabi* (the rust and patina of antique materials) and *wabi* (quietness and solitude) can provide the inspiration for softly patinated neutral surfaces and a still-life of pebbles by a bath or well. In a similar way, natural materials used in furnishings and a variety of plants and herbs arranged throughout an interior can bring a sense of the outside natural world indoors.

Just the act of travelling, of looking at another culture, can bring you home to look at your own life-style with different eyes. Many Westerners, used to being surrounded by rooms full of furniture and furnishings, find that the clean, empty spaces of traditional Eastern rooms offer respite from hectic lifes, while others appreciate such interiors for their links with the spiritual philosophies of the East. The art of simplicity is like getting dressed for a special event. You may have a beautifully cut white suit dotted with delicate pearl buttons. The temptation is always to add a gold belt, a stunning pair of earrings and a jewelled necklace, yet too much ornamentation and detail will fight each other, drowning the tailored perfection of the suit. By applying a similar philosophy to your interiors you will be able to test the truth of the expression – less is more.

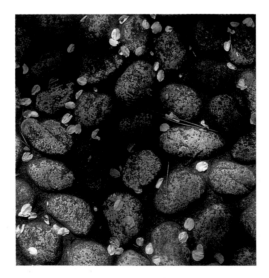

SIMPLICITY

A POOL SURROUNDED BY PEBBLES IS THE MOST
JAPANESE OF IMAGES, AND WOULD NORMALLY BE
FOUND OUTSIDE THE TEA-CEREMONY ROOM.
THE LINK BETWEEN WATER, CONTEMPLATION AND
PEACE HAS SPIRITUAL CONNOTATIONS, AND
THE IDEA OF USING WATER AS A DECORATIVE
FEATURE DOES NOT HAVE TO BE RESTRICTED TO
GARDENS OR SWIMMING POOLS. HOPPEN MAKES
THE MOST OF THE WATER ASSOCIATIONS TO
BE FOUND IN A BATHROOM AND EVOKES IMAGES
OF THE TEA-CEREMONY POOL BY SURROUNDING A
BATH (FAR LEFT) WITH PEBBLES. NOTE, TOO, THE
CONTRAST BETWEEN NATURAL STONE – THE
PEBBLES – AND STONE THAT HAS BEEN FINISHED BY
MAN – THE POLISHED BLACK TILES. FOR A MORE
SOPHISTICATED STILL-LIFE AROUND A SWIMMING
POOL, SHE TAKES A CONTEMPORARY SCULPTURE
AND A WICKER DIVAN AND PLACES THEM SO
THAT THEIR IMAGES ARE REFLECTED IN THE
STILL WATERS BELOW.

THE DESIGN ELEMENTS

WALLS

THE CONTRAST BETWEEN PLAIN WALLS AND INTRICATELY WORKED ARCHITECTURAL ELEMENTS, SUCH AS THIS DETAIL OF WROUGHT-IRONWORK (FAR RIGHT) FROM THE SULEIMAN MOSQUE IN ISTANBUL, IS TYPICAL OF MANY ASIAN AND MIDDLE EASTERN BUILDINGS, AND HOPPEN BORROWS THIS CONCEPT TO ADD AN EXOTIC FEEL TO HER INTERIORS. THE FOLDING DOORS OF A WOODEN LATTICEWORK SCREEN (LEFT) FROM VIETNAM CAN BE USED AS A FLEXIBLE WALL TO REDEFINE THE SPATIAL ORGANIZATION OF A ROOM. IT CAN ALSO CREATE AN UNUSUAL WINDOW TREATMENT. THE SUN STREAMS THROUGH THE DELICATELY CARVED WOOD IN INTRICATE PATTERNS, CASTING LIGHT AND SHADOW ACROSS THE ROOM AND ACHIEVING BOTH PRIVACY AS WELL AS A STRIKING VISUAL EFFECT. THESE DOORS CAN BE SECURED AT EITHER SIDE OF THE WINDOW AND USED AS SHUTTERS, OR EMPLOYED AS A FREE STANDING SCREEN, TO BE MOVED IN FRONT OF THE WINDOWS ON VERY BRIGHT DAYS. THE ORNATE PATTERN OF THIS SCREEN IS OFFSET BY THE SIMPLICITY OF ELEMENTS IN THE FOREGROUND. HERE HOPPEN HAS CHOSEN A VERY DISTINCTIVE THIRTIES-STYLE, ITALIAN-DESIGNED STOOL, IN WHICH THE CURVE OF THE SEAT AND STAND ECHO THE CURVACEOUS ARABESQUES OF THE LATTICE-WORK. AGAIN, A RESTRAINED PALETTE ALLOWS THE ATTENTION TO REST ON THE SHAPE AND DETAIL OF EACH OBJECT.

When creating the East meets West look, walls, windows and furnishings are your building blocks, and simplicity is the key. Walls provide the background for any interiors scheme and wall treatments which bring with them colour and texture will play a large part in determining the feel of a room. In the East, as in many Western cultures, homes are traditionally constructed from what is most plentifully offered by the land around. Local materials, such as wood, straw, earth, clay, bamboo or paper, provide an immediate source of colour and texture, creating a natural and organic framework. Pattern follows function and the rice-paper sliding walls of the archetypal Japanese home create a grid-system of simple planes while a brocaded curtain or a wooden latticework screen does double duty as door and decoration in an Indian home. But simple does not have to mean plain – consider the intricate detailing in the white plaster walls of a Hindu temple, the scalloped stone-work of a Venetian archway or the cross-beamed slats of burnished cedarwood in a Japanese ceiling – yet there is a sense of order to everything.

Wall colours in East-West style echo the natural hues of wood and clay, the silvery sheen of antique metal, and the calm off-whites of limewash and plaster. Rooms are based on neutral, relaxed backgrounds of white or cream, punctuated in a restrained manner with Japanese-style hangings or Western prints arranged on an oriental grid. As well as soft, pure white, textured natural tones reminiscent of stone, ivory, calico and parchment work well too, deepening to taupe, ochre and terracotta. Such neutral backgrounds are as flexible as the people who live with them. The atmosphere can be turned around in an instant by adding a carefully chosen Paisley pattern, a striking leopard print or a two-tone stripe, a pile of giant jewel-coloured cushions or a rich oriental throw.

A plain white wall, however, is more complex than it seems. Historic whites look like dull beige next to the twentieth-century's brilliant whites. The whiteness of tone is dependent on the percentage of optical brighteners used, and those with a low level – or none at all – look softer. Tones of white also vary according to the medium or material. With paint, for example, the different textures of eggshell, matt, gloss or emulsion will alter the shade, just as roughly textured slub linen will appear different to a smooth silk, a translucent sheer or a complex weave. White on white works beautifully, as does white on cream, and using these textural differences prevents the look from becoming dull. White-painted walls combined with furnishings and fittings in natural materials, such as wood, linen, wicker, terracotta and marble, will appear warmer and softer than a white background used as a contrast for bright colour.

KELLY HOPPEN TAKES THE CONCEPT OF A SCREEN ONE STEP FURTHER BY CREATING A 'BROKEN' WALL BETWEEN AN EN SUITE BATHROOM AND A BEDROOM. ORIGINALLY TWO ROOMS, SHE REPLACED THE ORIGINAL WALL WITH A HALF-WALL, INSET WITH GLASS-FREE OPENINGS THAT ALSO OFFER ORNAMENTAL STORAGE SPACE FOR PERFUME BOTTLES AND POTS. THIS WALL TREATMENT, AS SEEN IN RAJASTHAN (RIGHT), IS COMMON IN TROPICAL CLIMATES, AS IT ALLOWS MORE LIGHT AND MOVEMENT BETWEEN ROOM AREAS WHILST ALSO PROVIDING GOOD VENTILATION.

Neutral is not the only choice, however. And the quality and quantity of natural light as well as the size of a room are also important considerations. Oriental homes make great use of the 'broken wall', be it in the form of a sliding screen or a pierced lattice – a decorative feature that can be used to great effect when you need to orchestrate space without hindering the passage of light from one side of a room to the other. A dividing wall broken with squares of light will separate two rooms and still retain a sense of privacy. This device can be used in a number of situations: between bedroom and bathroom, kitchen and dining room, or to separate part of a living room that has been carved out for a home office.

A huge room with sunlight streaming in from large studio windows will look stunning in white, while a small, north-facing room with a single window may look cold and dark. To make the most of a small space, use all the available light and, if using pale colours, select either off-whites or creams which are warmer in tone than pure white. Or why not opt for a more dramatic approach with a rich saturated colour? Small rooms are often the ones which benefit most from major statements of colour and style – opening the door onto a brilliant Chinese-red bathroom creates a refreshing counterpoint to a predominantly neutral interior scheme. Splashes of exuberant colour are as much a part of Western style as that of the East and there is a rich inheritance to draw on – from jewel

THE NATURAL DRAPE OF INEXPENSIVE MATERIALS,

SUCH AS THE COTTON STRIPS HUNG FROM

THESE LOOMS IN INDIA, IS GRACEFUL IN ITSELF.

HOPPEN USES BOLTS OF PLAIN CALICO, FALLING

ABUNDANTLY TO THE FLOOR, AS THE ONLY

WALL DECORATION IN A SMALL AND SIMPLE

DINING ROOM. THESE WHITE BANNERS ARE

EFFECTIVE AS WELL AS FLEXIBLE – SIMPLY SEWN

ONTO A FABRIC COVERED WALL, IN TURN STAPLED

TO WOODEN BATTENS BENEATH, THEY CAN BE

EASILY CHANGED OR REMOVED.

reds, racing and empire greens, bold topaz blues and dramatic drawing-room yellows – found throughout Europe from traditional English country houses to bright Mediterranean interiors. Such colours can be borrowed from history to work beautifully – albeit in judicious amounts – within East-West decorative schemes, acting like punctuation points to the whole house, providing an essential contrast, and all the more delightful for being unexpected.

Textured paint effects give depth to neutral creams and white, and break up strong colours, softening the harshness of a large expanse of flat paint and recreating the weathered but brilliant effects to be found on the colourful walls of Indian or Moroccan houses, or walls glimpsed through the open door of an old palazzo in Venice. Chinese red, terracotta, deep emerald green and dark blue all gain depth from a simple paint treatment such as colourwashing, or colourwashing over sponging. Adding a few coats of varnish increases the depth and tonal qualities of the colour still further.

Fabric can be used on walls to create an extra dimension – that of texture – and it is a particularly successful means of introducing an opulent effect with a minimal use of colour. Fabric walls have a long lineage that extends from the tapestry-covered walls of Elizabethan times to the wall hangings of the eighteenth century which might have been velvet during the winter and taffeta or silk damask during the summer. They were often chosen to coordinate with the upholstery of the furniture. Indian painted cottons, or European printed imitations, and Chinese painted silk taffetas, known as *pékins*, were also favourites. These ravishing materials were seen in the most affluent houses including Mme de Pompadour's small chateau, Bellevue, in which all the furnishings were upholstered in *pékins* of various colours. In a similar way, colourful kilims used as wall hangings recall the nineteenth-century fascination with all things oriental. Historically, wall hangings were usually nailed to a framework of wooden battens, which in turn were fixed to the walls with nails which were then masked by a border or fillet (these were made primarily of wood, which was carved and gilded and later painted, but they were occasionally made of other materials like gilded leather). Modern means of construction are not dissimilar, but a staple gun can stand in for hammer and nails.

Linen is a contemporary equivalent for fabric-covered walls in the East-West interior. Equally, you could use a tartan check to echo a plaid sofa or a warm tartan rug tucked into a deep armchair. A fabric wall will give a very different feeling to one that is merely covered in wallpaper, and it also offers better coverage for walls that are pitted

FABRIC CAN BE USED TO CREATE DRAMATIC EFFECTS ON WALLS OR ON A MORE PRACTICAL LEVEL TO COVER UP UNSIGHTLY IMPERFECTIONS. FOR A SPARE ROOM (LEFT), HOPPEN USES A BOLT OF TARTAN HUNG CASUALLY OVER AN IRON POLE AS AN ELEGANT BED CANOPY – A TREATMENT WHICH REQUIRES THE MINIMUM OF ARRANGEMENT. FABRIC, LIKE THIS INEXPENSIVE MATTRESS TICKING (RIGHT), CAN BE USED TO GIVE A STYLISH FINISH TO WALLS. IT IS A COST-EFFECTIVE ALTERNATIVE TO WALLPAPER AND PAINT EFFECTS, AND CAN EITHER BE GLUED TO THE WALL OR FIXED WITH A STAPLE GUN.

with imperfections. Hessian, ticking or inexpensive upholstery linen can all be glued or stapled onto poor quality walls producing an immediate transformation, and upholstery techniques such as edging with bias binding or webbing create unusual effects when applied to walls. Such upholstery techniques will give a particularly tailored look when applied around wall niches (another favourite display area in Indian and Japanese homes), providing the finishing touches for the perfect display alcove.

An effective, and instant, facelift for a room can be achieved by using fabric banners – sheets of ironed calico or linen stapled to the top of the walls and allowed to hang to the floor. (In Japanese homes they employ a similar means of decoration by hanging narrow cotton banners, known as *nobori*, along the wall.) These wide strips of fabric, hung at regular intervals, echo the elegant decorative effect of Chinese calligraphic scrolls, which would be hung vertically on a wall, their fluid, cursive inscriptions penned with silver-powdered mica, usually on a paper or silk scroll. Easily rolled up, they could be stored when not in use and rearranged as required for particular occasions. Alternative decorative techniques employing fabric banners include a simple fall of fabric, hung as a canopy. Used in a bedroom or over a divan, this treatment can soften a restrained scheme, perhaps conjuring romantic images of a medieval jousting tent while still retaining an understated atmosphere.

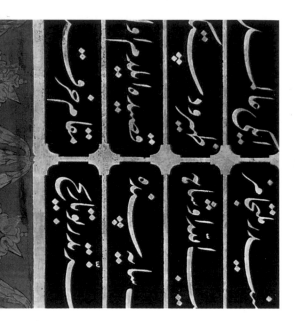

CALLIGRAPHY IS BOTH ART AND POETRY –
FROM THE ISLAMIC SCRIPT IN THE TOPKAPI PALACE
IN ISTANBUL (LEFT) TO A JAPANESE SCROLL
(RIGHT). BY REPEATING MOTIFS (NOTE HOW THE
CALLIGRAPHY ON THE SCROLL IS ECHOED IN
THE ELEGANT SCRIPT ON THE CHAIR UPHOLSTERY),
HOPPEN IS ABLE TO UNIFY A ROOM
CONTAINING DIFFERENT OBJECTS AND INFLUENCES
FROM ALL AROUND THE WORLD.
THIS TABLEAU IS CONTROLLED BY REPETITION
AND BY THE UNDERSTATED BACKGROUND
OF THE WALLS.

Walls create the chance to display collections and favourite objects. In fact, such pieces can become the starting point for the decoration of a whole room. There is a different attitude to display in the East, one that does not accord with traditional Western style where display cases and groups of pictures are expected to be found on every wall, and pictures are sometimes hung merely to fill a space. Eastern philosophy dictates that even if a picture, a mirror or a basket is purely decorative, it is placed in a position judiciously and for a very specific purpose. In Japan and China, works of art and calligraphic scrolls are switched around regularly according to the season, the day or even the visitor expected. There is a belief that looking at the same treasured possessions makes your mind stale. If a Western home has twenty pictures, you would expect most of them to be on the wall, and they will probably stay in place until the next move or major redecoration. Conversely, a traditional Japanese home may have twenty decorative scrolls, but only one or two will be on display at any one time, and a new arrangement might be expected every few weeks.

Wall space can also be an invaluable storage commodity. Whatever their background and culture, most families now have more possessions than previous generations. An increasing number of people work from home and need to store boxes, files and reference books. People need space for their passions, whether it is a collection of fifty pairs of shoes or a set of golf clubs. And all this in a world where space is increasingly at a premium. Clever ways need to be found to store possessions without stealing any more living space than is necessary.

WALLS

Most traditional Western storage has been achieved through furniture: the chest of drawers, the wardrobe and the dresser have been used in Western homes for centuries. In Eastern homes, however, there is less formal storage and possessions may be hung on hooks or stored in baskets. In a world without drawers or cupboards an orderly display of knives, brushes or other household necessities becomes a work of art in itself. Pots and baskets, or boxes and files may be ornamental in that they have beautiful, simple lines, but they also have a practical function. Repetition and organization are the key to this look: a whole wall of white-painted shelves demonstrates how wall storage can become part of the decorative scheme. By filling them with natural-coloured boxes in ascending sizes, you can achieve a look that is calm and orderly, whilst hiding any amount of chaos and mis-matching. The lines of the shelves themselves, both upright and horizontal, can become part of the overall pattern.

The range of possibilities for decorating walls East-West style are numerous, but this is a style that strives for simplicity and order. As such, it will work in any kind of architectural context, from the contemporary minimalism and bare brick of the New York loft to the most modest family home. It is also a look that stands the test of time and remains outside the giddy swings of the fashion cycle, evading the condemnation of the date stamp.

NEATLY PACKAGED BOXES IN A JAPANESE
CUPBOARD (RIGHT) OFFER INSPIRATION FOR A
HOME OFFICE. HOPPEN USES THE WHOLE OF THE
WALL SPACE AS A STORAGE AREA FOR A WIDE
RANGE OF DIFFERENTLY SIZED BOXES AND FILES.
ALL THE COLOURS ARE KEPT WITHIN A STRICTLY
NEUTRAL PALETTE, WITH PLAIN WHITE WALLS AND
CREAM BOXES AND FILES. THE KEY TO THE
SUCCESS OF THIS SCHEME IS THE EMPHASIS ON
TEXTURE – THE CONTRAST BETWEEN DIFFERENT
MATERIALS LIKE LEATHER AND CARDBOARD,
METAL AND WOOD – RATHER THAN COLOUR.
WITHIN SUCH A SMALL SPACE, ANY PATTERN OR
COLOUR, HOWEVER RIGOROUSLY COORDINATED,
CAN QUICKLY DETERIORATE INTO MUDDLE.

WALLS

WINDOWS

FULL-LENGTH LINEN CURTAINS ARE GIVEN A
GEOMETRIC TREATMENT WITH DEEP BORDERS.
PLAIN LINEN BLINDS HUNG BEHIND THE CURTAINS
ARE TREATED IN ORIENTAL STYLE WITH KNOTTED
BLACK TIES, WHICH EMPHASIZE THE WINDOWS'
NATURAL LINES AND CREATE A STRONG GRAPHIC
EFFECT. TIES CAN BE MADE OF SILK, VELVET, OR
COTTON IN A CONTRASTING COLOUR, AND ARE
THEN TIED OR KNOTTED TO HOLD THE LIFTED
BLIND IN PLACE. WRAP THE BLIND AROUND
A CARDBOARD TUBE TO KEEP IT NEATLY FURLED.

The window treatments typical of Japan, China and India are traditionally simpler than those in Western homes. From medieval times onwards, curtains and bed hangings have been used in Western houses for decoration and insulation. However, in contemporary interiors there has been a reaction against over-the-top curtains and elaborate window treatments in favour of a cleaner, more defined look. The East meets West style approaches windows in two distinct ways: either by taking the simplicity of the oriental blind and adding a unique twist like a rich velvet knot, or by adapting the luscious fabrics of traditional European windows and simplifying them into a more controlled, restrained look.

In the West, fabric has been a major element in status and style in a way that has not been equalled in the East despite the fact that north-west Europe and Japan have similar climates – indeed Japan is often considerably colder. Yet while European homes have often been fortresses against inclement weather, the traditional Japanese country house used sliding doors and walls to blur the distinction between outside and inside. In Europe heavy drapes and hangings, tapestries and brocades have delineated wealth and rank since the fifteenth century, yet in Japan a simple panel of finely woven silk might be considered fit for an emperor. And while silk was prized as a luxury item and a mark of personal wealth in China, it was never draped around windows and doors. Many French styles – ornate neoclassical pelmets, elaborate swagged and gilded cornices and scalloped or festooned valances topping lavish windows of silk – came to influence Western interior design. The concept of a window treatment as a main focal point for a room spread throughout northern Europe, and

WINDOWS

even today only the mantelpiece or fireplace has more decorative importance. It is this relatively lavish style that has dominated windows in the West up to the present day.

The traditional bamboo or rattan blind, simply hung from a window and scrolled up or down against the sun's rays, can be found everywhere in the East from India to Tibet, Thailand to Japan. Inexpensive and effective, this kind of blind is equally at home in a minimalist contemporary room, a rustic farmhouse setting or as a peaceful backdrop to a more luxurious interior, being warmer and more organic than metal Venetian blinds. It is easy to get so carried away with the decorative side of window treatments that you forget their primary function, which is to control light and add privacy. Bamboo and rattan blinds, so evocative of hot tropical climates, and the simplest, most authentic East-West window treatment, gently filter strong light by day, but when rooms are lit by artificial light at night they provide little privacy. If this is a problem, you will need to line them with fabric. Alternatively, translucent materials – linen, cotton and sheers such as muslin – can be used to filter light, and are more effective at providing privacy. A plain fabric blind, pulled halfway up the window, is a more relaxed way of shielding an ugly view or the gaze of curious passers-by than net or lace curtains. In bedrooms the aim is often to block out light completely, from streetlamps or morning sun, until it is wanted, and for this you will need to line and interline blinds.

The principle of the textured, natural-toned rattan blind can be re-created in other materials – either cheaply in hessian or cotton, or luxuriously in linen and silk. One advantage of this is that rattan and bamboo darken in the sun, and require vacuuming rather than dry cleaning, so fabric options may be easier to maintain. Roman blinds, with their graceful folds of fabric lapping over each other in an understated way, are a particularly attractive alternative. Simpler variations of pull-up blinds also make the most of the way the material falls and they rarely have ruching or complex folds. With blinds like these the focus is on the subtle hues and textures of the fabric, such as knobbly slub silk or rough-woven linen. Fabric blinds are also a good solution to unusually shaped windows – those that are curved at the top, for example, where you can echo the canopies of St Mark's Square in Venice with blinds that follow the line of the curve. Whether you have a flat casement window or a traditional sash window, a blind will leave the shape and size of the window exposed, and by using blinds on their own you can save space – tiny country houses or crowded studies look less cluttered without voluminous folds of fabric.

RATTAN, BAMBOO AND ALL KINDS OF BASKET-WEAVE ARE EVOCATIVE OF TRADITIONAL LIFE THROUGHOUT ASIA, LIKE THESE FISHTRAPS (RIGHT) BEING WOVEN OUT OF LOCAL REED BY A CAMBODIAN GIRL. HOPPEN UTILIZES THE TEXTURE OF RATTAN FOR BEDROOM BLINDS (INSET). BLINDS ARE MORE PRACTICAL FOR SMALL WINDOWS, ESPECIALLY IN ROOMS WHERE SPACE IS AT A PREMIUM. A MORE EXOTIC EFFECT IS ACHIEVED WITH A BLACK RATHER THAN A NATURAL-COLOURED BLIND (ABOVE), AND THIS IS COMPLEMENTED BY A GIANT ENGRAVED HOOK WHICH WOULD ORIGINALLY HAVE BEEN USED FOR HANGING MOSQUITO NETS. SUCH UNUSUAL ACCESSORIES ADD AN ORIENTAL TOUCH OF MYSTERY TO A STILL-LIFE COMPOSITION.

WINDOWS

NEW TRICKS WITH OLD LOOKS: HOPPEN GIVES
ANTIQUE CURTAINS A NEW LEASE OF LIFE BY
HANGING THEM AT A BEDROOM WINDOW
(FAR LEFT) IN COMBINATION WITH A LINEN BLIND.
NEITHER THE PELMET NOR THE CURTAINS WERE
CUT DOWN TO SIZE. INSTEAD THE PELMET RUNS
ACROSS THE WIDTH OF TWO WINDOWS AND
THE CURTAINS CASCADE TO THE FLOOR. ALTERNA-
TIVELY, SHE MAY USE TASSELS ON SIMPLE BLINDS
(LEFT), OR CREATE A DRAMATIC LOOK WITH
THE SWEEPING LINES OF HUGE VELVET CURTAINS
(OVERLEAF). FOR AN OPULENT DRAPE THE
CURTAINS ARE PULLED CLOSED AT THE TOP WITH
TIE-BACKS POSITIONED LOW TO ACHIEVE MAXIMUM
FULLNESS. THE DEEP INDIGO BLUE OF A JAPANESE
KIMONO IS ECHOED IN THE COLOUR SCHEME.

Fully lined Roman blinds can be used effectively on their own or behind curtains. The combination of a blind placed behind a curtain works well with more elaborate window treatments, as the blind can be simply pulled up or dropped down with the minimum of fuss, without disturbing the careful arrangement of fragile or antique textiles. Once again, neutral or natural shades will act as a foil for the colour or pattern of the main curtain treatment. Blinds used in this way can preserve fabrics beyond their normal lifespan, as drawing curtains backwards and forwards and constantly rearranging them creates most of the wear and tear. A blind will also help to protect delicate curtain fabrics from the damaging effects of the sun.

The blind, used either on its own or in conjunction with more luxurious curtains, is the most atmospheric East-West window treatment. The simplicity of the blind does not necessarily mean that the resulting window treatment will be boring, and discreet decorative touches like banding or unusual knots or tassels, used as a means of tying up blinds, lift a window treatment out of the ordinary. For blinds that remain half-dropped and in the same position most of the time, you might like to add smart

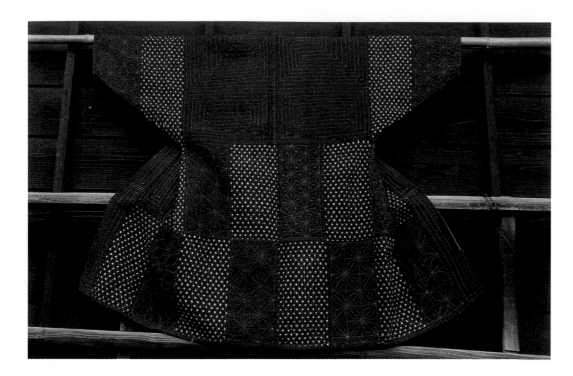

ties in contrasting black or navy, reminiscent of a kimono belt. These ties can be fixed about one quarter of the way down the blind on either side, and will tie up beneath in an elaborate knot. Other unusual touches might include a mosquito hook wound into the tie, adding a glint of metal and a whisper of the East. For decorative touches on blinds that are raised and lowered more often, giant tassels along the bottom, or on either side of the pelmet, add a touch of luxury without too much fussiness. Another good trick is to add a broad band of dark contrasting edging: navy or black with cream blinds, or perhaps cream against natural taupe-coloured linen.

Cross-fertilization is always inspirational, and there is scope for adapting the luxury of Western curtain treatments and enjoying them in a more Eastern manner. Window treatments, above all, should be appropriate to the architecture of the house, and many generously proportioned European windows were designed with indulgent curtains in mind. By contrast, a city in China will have street after street of private, blank walls, while windows face inwards to courtyards and gardens. Equally, in a Japanese home the vast sliding doors, which act as substitutes for windows, would look inappropriate if obstructed by masses of drapery. Western-style architecture demands an emphasis on window treatments because large, light windows are one of a house's greatest assets.

WINDOWS

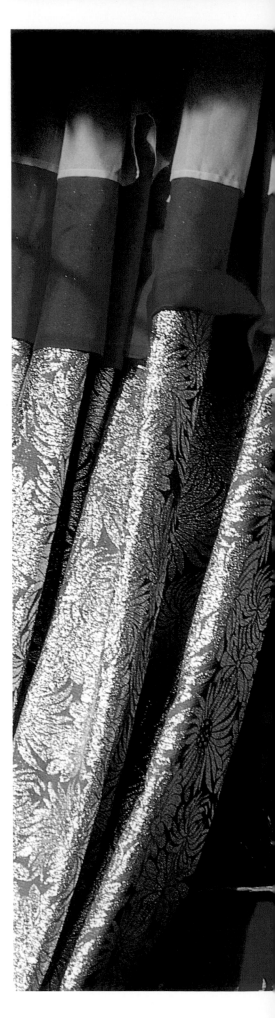

BALINESE TEMPLE OFFERINGS (FAR RIGHT) ARE SCREENED BY A DRAPE DEFINED WITH A VIBRANT PELMET. HOPPEN USES BANDING TO CREATE TWO DIFFERENT CURTAIN TREATMENTS: LINEN CURTAINS WITH DEEP BORDERS ARE HELD BACK BY OMBRAS (ABOVE) WHILST A BANDED FABRIC DRAPED OVER A CURTAIN POLE ACTS AS A PELMET (RIGHT).

If you choose curtains rather than blinds, check that the room is large enough to accommodate the fabric without a sense of over-crowding. Floor-length curtains may be appropriate for large windows, but in the recessed windows of a small cottage they will obscure the room's features, so curtains just inside or over the window-ledge level are more suitable. At the other end of the spectrum, a full set of curtains offers a chance to be lavish. By lengthening curtains beyond floor level you can enjoy the graceful swirl of fabric on the floor. This is a good trick to remember if you have an old house which has settled slightly, as the floors and walls are often uneven and the mounds of fabric can be used to obscure this imperfection. The fullness of the curtain is important too – a rough rule of thumb for curtains is to measure two-and-a-half times the width of the window, but if you are hanging a single drape at each window, pulled back to one side, then one-and-a-half times the width will be sufficient.

Curtains can be made in virtually any fabric, but natural materials such as linen, silk, cotton, calico or velvet suit the philosophy of this decorating style best. Once again, most of the emphasis comes from the texture and drape of the fabric, plus a few additional decorative touches. Curtains and blinds in plain colours tend to be more practical than a riot of florals or a toile de Jouy, however pretty. Unpatterned fabrics can still be just as luxurious – think of thick, rich blue velvet curtains draped luxuriously behind curtain bosses, or dressed up with giant tassels holding them back. They can be hung liberally at the window, or drawn back to make the most of the light. Colours like navy, cream, white or stone work well with a wide range of decorative styles. Try not to get too bound up in fussy curtain material with matching furnishings as you will lose that important element of flexibility.

It is possible to create particular points of interest by employing various accessories for curtains. Single but stunning decorative touches, like a contrasting band running down the edges of the curtain, will help to define the shape of a window, as well as lending definition to the fall of the fabric. Elaborate pelmet treatments are rarely used in this decorating style, as they crowd rather than accentuate the window's natural lines. If you have a complex pelmet treatment, you may well find that it refreshes the room simply to remove it and re-hang the curtains with a striking tie-back – it is a quick and simple way of adding light and updating the window arrangement. Think big when it comes to tie-backs, as giant tassels and carved wooden bosses or ombras can add a touch of grandeur or exoticism to the humblest of fabrics.

WINDOWS

However, all rules were made to be broken, and it is always refreshing to come across a visual surprise or a piece of self-indulgence, perhaps a patterned fabric which has been chosen because someone fell in love with it. There are several classic fabric styles with an Eastern feel – crewelwork and Paisley come from India, stripes are to be found everywhere from Constantinople to Japan, and there is a Chinese influence running through many chintzes. East meets West style is very much about blending influences from different parts of the world to find your own individual style. If you fall for a charming toile de Jouy from France, a stately English country chintz or a spriggy cottage print, you can either use them as a major statement in an otherwise neutral interior, or as the decorative feature that sets the theme for a smaller room, such as a downstairs cloakroom, breakfast room or spare bedroom.

Nothing is wasted in Eastern cultures, and this is a philosophy that can be utilized in Western homes. Instead of casting aside old fabrics and out-dated curtains, find ways of making them live again. Opulent does not have to mean extravagant and luxury does not necessarily spell wastefulness. Faded but exquisite brocade and velvet curtains can be re-hung and enjoyed in another room. Nothing is changed or damaged in the process. Instead of cutting down old curtain fabrics and re-stitching them – a process which could damage fragile fabric further, and would also mean that they would be unlikely to fit any other windows – simply hang them as they are, allowing the long swathes of luxurious fabric to flow to the floor, coiling in waves at the base. Even if you move house, there is no need to start again with completely new curtains – a tip for revamping and revitalizing an old pair of curtains is to add a contrasting broad band around the hem, pulling them back with silken ropes and tassels and perhaps adding a filmy sheer undercurtain. Dressed differently, a tired set of curtains can look stunning.

When dressing a window and choosing accessories it is important to always bear in mind the window's context in the scheme of each room. This should be your primary concern before choosing fabric, or deciding on decorative features such as pelmets or tie-backs. You will need to consider whether the window treatment is to be the focal point in a room, thus requiring a more unusual treatment, or whether you want it to remain unostentatious for maximum flexibility. The size and function of the window and the room are also important, as are the considerations of light and privacy. Once these functional aspects have been resolved you can concentrate on the more specific decorative details that will make your window treatment unique.

WINDOWS

THE RICHLY WORKED PATTERN OF AN ANTIQUE BOKHARA SUZANI CARPET (LEFT) IS EVIDENCE OF THE CRAFTS-
MANSHIP TO BE FOUND IN TRADITIONAL SKILLS. SIMILAR DETAIL CAN BE FOUND IN CREWELWORK, AN EMBROIDERY
STYLE CHARACTERIZED BY BOLD FLORAL DESIGNS THAT INSPIRED THESE INDIAN-PRINT CURTAINS (ABOVE).

FURNISHINGS

Furnishings, more than anything else in a home, reflect the life-style of the occupant, and they do not have to be rigorously themed or matched to make an interior that works. Whether passionate about Western antiques or hand-crafted furniture, this is a style that will incorporate beautiful pieces from China and India alongside classic Chippendale or Heppelwhite. It is here that East can really meet West to produce a look that is both individual and eclectic. Taking the best of other cultures does not mean discarding your own, and whether you live in the East or the West, the first step towards creating an interior that reflects your needs and life-style is to look at what you have in your house and, if necessary, redefine it. By redefining the traditional role of furnishings you can create an unusual slant to a room. Eastern life-styles tend to be less cluttered and more serene – in India, for example, cushions on the floor are used for seating so there is no great history of chairs. In Japan, interiors are calm, clear and orderly, lacking the abundance of decorative possessions which typify many Western homes. Chinese art and furniture can be fantastically decorative but there is none of the over-stuffed furniture and swathes of fabric that you might find in traditional English country houses. Furniture in the East tends to be multi-functional, while the West has a diverse range of pieces for each specific function and room: a bedroom chair, a dining-room chair and a sitting-room chair may all be distinctive and different.

Both Eastern and Western furniture and soft furnishings look to the natural world for inspiration – making the most of raw materials by leaving bare the texture of highly polished wood or woven matting, or seeking out and emphasizing their myriad patterns and colours. It is the mix that makes an interior exciting: the subtle clash, and resultant spark of electricity, that you get from the juxtaposition of a beautiful Renaissance painting above the clean lines of a contemporary cabinet, or a Chinese silk scroll hanging next to a nineteenth-century chest of drawers. A real home evolves over time, so nothing could be more natural than a blend of eras, tastes and styles.

Wood in all its forms – antique or contemporary, lovingly polished or smartly lacquered, beautifully inlaid or weathered and distressed – is central to the theme of East meets West. The furniture itself varies from continent to continent, and can be adapted for alternative uses in different cultures, but the tradition of craftsmanship links the two hemispheres together. It seems likely, for example, that the Western coffee table has been borrowed from the long, low tables of Japan, and a beautifully wrought Indian door, turned on its side,

FURNISHINGS

INTERESTING DETAILS ON CUSHIONS CAN LIFT A CHAIR OUT OF THE ORDINARY. A FRENCH SILVER-GILT CHAIR (LEFT) WOULD TRADITIONALLY HAVE BEEN UPHOLSTERED IN AN EXTRAVAGANT FABRIC, BUT BY USING A PLAIN CALICO, HOPPEN GIVES THE CHAIR A MORE CONTEMPORARY APPEAL. TO FINISH OFF THE COMPOSITION SHE USES CUSHION COVERS MADE FROM ANTIQUE MATTRESS TICKING, FASTENED WITH VICTORIAN PEARL BUTTONS. A BURMESE WEDDING BASKET BECOMES AN UNUSUAL SIDE TABLE, AND DESPITE DIFFERENT CULTURAL ORIGINS ALL THESE ELEMENTS SIT COMFORTABLY TOGETHER. OTHER DECORATIVE EFFECTS FOR CUSHIONS INCLUDE TIES IN A CONTRASTING PAISLEY FABRIC AND CRISS-CROSSED BINDINGS (ABOVE).

KELLY HOPPEN USES A LEATHER THEME TO DRAW TOGETHER THE ELEMENTS OF THIS LIVING ROOM (LEFT), GIVING THE IMPRESSION THAT IT IS THE HOME OF A WELL-SEASONED TRAVELLER. THE ANTIQUE SUITCASES AND THE VINTAGE GOYARD TRUNK ARE MULTI-FUNCTIONAL AND DOUBLE-UP AS STORAGE AND COFFEE TABLES, WHILE THE LEATHER BOOKS AND HAT BOX PICK UP THE THEME. THE CHAIRS AROUND THE BAR ARE UPHOLSTERED IN ALCANTARA, A VERY REALISTIC (BUT WASHABLE) SUEDE-LOOK FABRIC, WHICH MAKES SUCH EXTRAVAGANT MATERIALS A PRACTICAL OPTION. A SINGLE CHAIR (ABOVE) PLACED IN FRONT OF A WINDOW CAN ACT AS AN IMPROMPTU SIDE TABLE. THE CLASSIC REGENCY STRIPES ON THE CHAIR SEAT COMPLEMENT THE STYLE OF THE CHAIR, AND AS THE SUN STREAMS THROUGH THE WINDOW, SILHOUETTING ITS SHAPE, YOUR ATTENTION IS INSTANTLY DRAWN TO ITS ELEGANT LINES.

makes a beautiful dining table or coffee table. Side tables can be fashioned from almost anything from a lacquered rice basket to a pile of books. Leather Vuitton suitcases and trunks, lacquered Burmese rice baskets and circular cherrywood commode chests are all the right shape and size, and with their atmosphere of travel to faraway places, are more interesting and stylish than the standard side table.

Start with your major pieces of furniture – sofas, beds, dining tables. What function do you need them to fulfil? How big should they be? Can you have different furniture for each room or do you need to retain fluidity of movement between the rooms in order to move a chair from a bedroom to a living room or dining room as the need dictates? You may prefer to have your private life and public entertaining spaces separated by completely different decorative styles, but as entertaining becomes less formal and space more limited, the concept of special rooms or furniture is quickly declining. Both the dining room and the drawing room, once essential rooms and the only part of the house that visitors would have seen, have now been amalgamated in many homes to form a multi-functional living space.

Think big, even in small rooms. One over-sized piece of furniture is a way of creating impact, and is often more practical than a smaller piece. A generous three- or four-seater sofa takes up little more space than a two-seater, but accommodates more people in greater comfort. Two little side tables simply look cluttered, while one low, long table has an air of grandeur and offers a greater expanse of usable surface. Flexible furnishings such as a spare chair, chest or mirror can be set against a wall, or in a corner or a corridor as the centre of its own still-life composition: a chair, a painting, two cushions and a rice basket, arranged so that they are a pleasure to look at and are on hand for use when needed. Redefining tradition means using your furniture in different ways, but it does not mean trying to find a space for everything. If you do not need something and you do not love it, find some other home for it. Having decided on your major pieces of furniture for each room, there are usually only one or two obvious locations to site them. Sofas can be focused around a fireplace or coffee table, and beds should be situated away from wardrobes and chests of drawers. Having decided on the overall colour scheme, the walls and the window treatments, the bones of the room are in place and you can now begin to build atmosphere as if you were painting a picture, adding and changing accents and detail according to changes in season, fashion or life-style.

FURNISHINGS

Lights and lighting are also part of a room's 'furniture' and are an essential element in creating the right kind of atmosphere. For this reason, the lighting in a room should be planned at the earliest possible stage. Many people feel that they cannot plan the lighting until they have decided on their furniture layout, but a general lighting scheme that will cover all eventualities is a sensible precaution to take. There are usually only one, two, or at the most, three positions for a sofa or a bed in a room, and it is wise to position plugs and wall lights so that you can change the room around if you want to. In small spaces, wall lights and uplighters can be very effective as well as practical, avoiding the need for lamps and side tables, while the installation of dimmer switches means that you can alter the mood in seconds. Central pendant lighting has fallen out of favour in recent years, but it can be an opportunity for a dramatic statement, perhaps using an upturned shade which throws light up towards the ceiling and creates a gentler, more flattering atmosphere. This can be achieved with a wide variety of looks: classic Thirties shades, contemporary paper shades, or extravagant Fortuny fabric shades.

Soft furnishings, such as sofa covers and upholstered chairs, offer tremendous scope for creativity, but once again it is important to stand back and ask yourself what you want from the overall scheme before getting involved in the merits of buttons over hooks or braid over binding. 'Less is more' in the East-West philosophy and fewer, larger pieces with clean lines and plain or textured fabrics work better than a collection of small, but cumbersome pieces of furniture. Big, upholstered pieces can then act as a continuation of the canvas that includes walls, curtain treatments, ceilings and floors, or they can be highlights, adding a sense of surprise and drama, and standing alone as focal points. A sofa, for example, in natural shades of cream, oatmeal, stone, ivory, charcoal, or taupe, can alter its personality in an instant with throws or cushions. Alternatively, it can have a major impact, upholstered in vibrant purple velvet, as the main splash of colour in the room. Either way works well, but if your main colour statement comes from the sofa, you will probably have to be careful how much – or how little – you crowd the space around it with similar colour. Either go all the way – a small, dark emerald-green study can be as cosy as a green cocoon, with walls and furnishings in similar tones – or introduce one dramatic piece in a muted room otherwise full of taupe, metallic silver and soft greys. This avoids the cliché of the matching three-piece suite and curtains – an obvious nightmare in purple velvet, and drab and predictable in less exciting fabrics – being neither 'less' nor 'more'.

SOFTER AND MORE FLUID THAN LAMPSHADES, AND OFTEN MORE DECORATIVE, LANTERNS – LIKE THESE NEATLY ARRANGED ROWS IN A JAPANESE SHOP (TOP RIGHT) – ARE TO BE FOUND THROUGH-OUT ASIA. THEIR DELICATE TRACERY AND THE STARK CONTRAST BETWEEN LIGHT AND DARK IS ECHOED IN HOPPEN'S ORIENTAL-INSPIRED LIGHTING. CHARACTER CAN BE ADDED TO FEATURELESS CEILINGS BY USING A STRIPED UPHOLSTERY FABRIC (BOTTOM RIGHT). SHE THEN HANGS A THIRTIES-INSPIRED BOWL PENDANT LIGHT FROM A CENTRAL POINT. THE DENSE COLOURED GLASS THROWS OUT A DIFFUSE LIGHT – NOT JUST THROUGH THE GLASS SIDES, BUT ALSO BOUNCED UP ONTO THE CEILING – AND FOUR SHADOWS THROWN OUT FROM THE CENTRE CREATE THE ILLUSION OF A TENT, ESPECIALLY WHEN COMBINED WITH THE STRIPED FABRIC. HOWEVER, PENDANT LIGHTS COME IN MANY DIFFERENT SHAPES AND STYLES, AND A TOTALLY DIFFERENT EFFECT IS ACHIEVED WITH THE GIANT SWIRL OF A SILK FORTUNY SHADE (TOP LEFT). THE BLACK FILIGREE EFFECT ON THE SHADE AND THE ELEGANT TASSEL EMULATE AN ORIENTAL PARASOL. PENDANT LIGHTS ARE IDEAL FOR THOSE WHO DISLIKE THE STRONG TRIANGULAR POOL OF LIGHT THROWN DOWN BY TRADITIONAL LAMPSHADES. IF SIDE LIGHTING IS PREFERRED, HOPPEN LOOKS FOR AN UNUSUAL SLANT ON A TRADITIONAL IDEA – FORTUNY LAMPS (BOTTOM LEFT), HANGING FROM A STAND, LOOK LIKE SILKEN LANTERNS AND ILLUMINATE THE ROOM WITH A SOFT GLOW.

FURNISHINGS

DETAILED CUSHIONS AND A STRIKING ROW OF
TOPIARY TREES ARE THE MAIN DECORATIVE
EMPHASIS FOR A LONG WINDOW-SEAT. DIFFERENT
SHAPES, SIZES AND MATERIALS ARE HIGHLIGHTED
AGAINST A NEUTRAL BACKGROUND OF NATURAL
CALICO, WHITE WALLS AND STRIPPED FLOOR-
BOARDS. FOR THE CUSHIONS HOPPEN MIXES
LUXURIOUS AND INEXPENSIVE MATERIALS – RED
VELVET AND PLAIN UPHOLSTERY LINEN – FOR
A CONTEMPORARY LOOK. DETAILING, SUCH AS
MOTHER-OF-PEARL BUTTONS AND CONTRASTING
BORDERS, ADD POINTS OF INTEREST. EASTERN
ELEMENTS ARE INTRODUCED THROUGH THE USE
OF EXTRAVAGANT EMBROIDERY, A STYLIZED
LIZARD MONOGRAM AND LENGTHS OF FABRIC
DRAPED OVER THE SEAT LIKE A BANNER, WHICH
COMBINE EASILY WITH WESTERN DECORATIVE
EFFECTS SUCH AS THE USE OF NEUTRAL LINEN
AND BOLSTER CUSHIONS.

Another good decorating trick which you can employ to good effect is to re-upholster traditional pieces of furniture in surprising ways, avoiding obvious choices. A beautiful cherrywood chair shows off its lines all the more clearly when decked in plain, humble cotton, calico or undyed linen. Inexpensive upholstery scrim combined with an elegant piece of furniture provides an unexpected textural contrast of rough fabric and polished wood. Beautiful furniture deserves first-class treatment, but that does not have to mean expensive materials. Quality shows up in workmanship and detailing too – it is better to spend money on a good upholsterer who will do the job well, and save by using honest, less expensive materials such as ticking, scrim or linen, to which you can then add unusual buttons or a contrasting binding to finish it off.

Attention to detail is the vital ingredient that lifts a pleasing interior out of the ordinary and makes it exciting. By using unusual materials and clever tricks you can make the most of cushions, bolsters and throws. Cushions can be extravagant in velvet and silk, in dramatic colours such as Chinese red or emerald green, or with a lovingly worked embroidered motif. Or they could be made of antique ticking or scrim and finished stylishly with binding and buttoning. Leather is another material to consider – a soft brown leather theme, repeated intermittently in a room, hints at expensive luggage and exotic destinations. For example, plain linen curtains can be banded with leather, or leather buttons can be added to cushions and the theme echoed in a row of leather-bound books. Or contrast linen and gold silk for an opulent feel, or linen and felt for a more textured look. You can create a whole theme for a room by picking two or three contrasting materials and re-using them in different forms, in the same way that a decorative scheme uses tones of contrasting colour.

Most people are familiar with runners as long thin carpets, adding accents to a hall or stairway – but runners can be adapted and used on furnishings, too. Taken from the Japanese *obi* or kimono sash, or the narrow banners known as *nobori*, you can add a decorative highlight with narrow strips of fabric on a sofa, curtain, table or bed. This is a good way of introducing pattern and colour in a controlled way: think of the effect of a deep red brocade stripe running down the centre of a cream armchair, a length of blue-and-white antique ticking on a white chair, or a favourite strip of fabric wrapped around a Victorian sofa.

The contrasting band is another favourite East-West device for cushions and soft furnishings, making a decorative impact through the juxtaposition of colours and textures. Leather and linen, silk and scrim, black and stone, navy and cream – each combination,

FURNISHINGS

in its own way, is both smart and sensual. An old, but loved bedspread can be given a new lease of life with a contrasting border of fabric around the edge – this is also a useful trick when you find an antique bedcover is too skimpy for a king-size bed. Alternatively, layered cushion covers provide an excellent opportunity for contrast, combining patterned fabric with plain, or cheap fabric with expensive. Try slipping a silk Fortuny cover over a cheap linen one, leaving the linen clearly exposed underneath, and button or tie the two together.

Buttons are very effective in conveying a smart, tailored look or a touch of discreet luxury. Try covering them in contrasting fabric like navy with white, or rifle through old haberdashery shops to find something special like mother-of-pearl or burnished metal. Buttons can also be used to tie bolsters – leave a 'pony tail' of fabric at each end and secure it with mother-of-pearl buttons or a handsome silk tie. Inexpensive materials with interesting surface textures, such as carpet bindings or humble Petersham ribbon, have attractive herringbone weaves and can be used as edging, a useful tip if you want to re-vamp cushions that look a little tired.

New ways of arranging furnishings can also add interest and an element of exoticism to a room. Rather than puffing up sofa cushions and arranging them at angles in a row, the ordered symmetry of a pile of Japanese floor cushions can be used as a starting point for a Western seating area. Cushions set one on top of the other, in order of descending size or in identical piles and rows, are quick and easy to arrange, and look stylish. The Eastern custom of big floor cushions adapts perfectly to the Western home, adding flexibility without cluttering up a room. A large divan, neatly piled Turkish-style with giant cushions, can act as a sofa or daybed that can be turned into an impromptu spare bed for guests. Diverse elements are brought together through repetition and symmetry, repeating a curved shape or colour several times over, and picking up a theme such as leather or stone, or a colour such as gold or black, and echoing it unexpectedly in several different places around the room.

This is a flexible attitude and accords all rooms in the house equal importance. Bedrooms and bathrooms are more private than living rooms and kitchens, but a rice basket sits as well in the former as in the latter. In this way, the East-West style enables you to look at and use traditional furnishings in a totally different way, incorporating all the elements and objects that make up a contemporary home. A house that reflects your personality should look stylish long after superficial design fashions have dated.

KELLY HOPPEN'S USE OF PATTERN IN SOFT FURNISHINGS IS CALM AND CONTROLLED. HER FAVOURITES INCLUDE TRADITIONAL PAISLEYS OR CHECKS THAT HAVE BOTH EASTERN AND WESTERN CONNOTATIONS. A RICH BROCADE RUNNER (ABOVE) ADDS A FLASH OF COLOUR TO A PLAINLY UPHOLSTERED CHAIR, BUT CAN ALSO BE REMOVED OR CHANGED FOR A DIFFERENT MOOD. HOWEVER, WHEN USING PATTERNED UPHOLSTERY FOR FURNISHINGS (LEFT), SHE PREFERS TO KEEP THE OTHER DECORATIVE ELEMENTS IN A ROOM, SUCH AS THE CURTAINS, LIGHT AND AIRY FOR A LOOK THAT IS NEITHER HEAVY NOR CONTRIVED. THIS ALLOWS THE BEAUTY OF THE WOODEN PANELLING TO SHOW THROUGH, AND A GIANT TASSEL AND CHECK CUSHIONS ADD AN EAST-WEST TOUCH OF LUXURY TO THE SCHEME.

FURNISHINGS

MANTELSCAPES

CHANGING THE MANTELSCAPE IS THE QUICKEST WAY TO REFRESH A ROOM. EACH MANTELSCAPE IS BASED ON A PARTICULAR PIECE, LIKE A CLASSICAL BUST OR A CHINESE FIGURINE (RIGHT), OR A COLOUR THEME, LIKE THE CONTRAST BETWEEN THE IVORY OF VELLUM BOOKS AND RED LACQUERWARE (BELOW). THE SUCCESS OF EACH COMPOSITION LIES IN THE CAREFUL ORCHESTRATION OF ELEMENTS ACCORDING TO COLOUR, SHAPE AND HEIGHT.

The design of the mantelpiece in Western homes has been the object of more creativity than almost any other single feature. Made in marble, stone, metal or wood, intricately carved or left plain, dominating the room or a modest statement, there is an infinite variety of styles and materials. There is also an equally varied number of ways of making the most of your mantelscape. On entering a room the mantelscape is often the first thing that you notice and changing it is one of the quickest and easiest ways of revitalizing an interior.

In Western houses, the fireplace is the focal point of a room just as Eastern homes are centered around the hearth. But whereas the one would be centrally placed on a wall, the other traditionally comprised an open fire sunk into the middle of the floor in a stone- or clay-lined pit. Charcoal was kept constantly burning, warming the suspended tea kettle throughout the day. The only decoration in this composition was the long, ornate pot hook, or *jizai-kagi*, which was tied to a beam in the ceiling. In Eastern homes the only feature comparable to the mantelpiece is the display alcove. Known as the *tokonoma* in Japan, these were places of daily prayer, erected in honour of the gods and ancestors that were responsible for the well-being of the family. As a tribute to the gods these household altars were lavishly decorated and, like a mantelpiece, provided a decorative focus.

Balance, repetition and attention to detail are the cornerstones of the East-West design philosophy, and are the three keys to a successful display of objects and treasures. Whether you love beautifully crafted antiques, brightly coloured china or simple

MANTELSCAPES

THESE MANTELSCAPES ARE BASED ON THE HARD, GLOSSY TEXTURES OF BOTH EASTERN AND WESTERN MATERIALS: GLASS, METAL, CELADON CERAMICS AND LACQUERWORK. THE CALLIGRAPHY BRUSHES (RIGHT) ADD A CONTRASTING TOUCH OF ORGANIC SOFTNESS.

Shaker-style artefacts, all are displayed effectively by instilling an Eastern sense of order. This does not mean that objects have to be rigidly matched and marshalled, simply that objects should be pared-down, shapes need to echo each other, sizes should be grouped together and curves counterbalanced with straight lines.

Start your composition with a bold piece, or your favourite object, and build the display up from there. The traditional European arrangement for a mantelscape starts with a central clock or statuette, followed by matching candlesticks and vases arranged equilaterally on either side. But by turning the look around, you can see how different effects can be achieved. Rather than a symmetrical arrangement, perhaps there is a striking bust with a fine profile which could be placed at one end, or alternatively a row of identical flowers in unusual or striking vases could be placed, equidistant from each other, along the mantel. The principles of asymmetrical balance work well when applied to displaying objects. Two large round black pots on the right-hand side of a mantel might be similar to, but not the same as, several smaller round black pots on the left-hand side. Look at your various elements in terms of the shape, volume and colour of the whole composition and not whether or not the pots match. In an asymmetrical arrangement objects need to be balanced, but not in

MANTELSCAPES

KELLY HOPPEN BEGINS EACH MANTELSCAPE
BY DECIDING ON A FOCAL POINT OR OBJECT, AND
THEN BUILDING THE COMPOSITION AROUND IT.
SHE WILL THEN DECIDE WHETHER TO FOLLOW A
SYMMETRICAL OR ASYMMETRICAL ARRANGEMENT,
CONSIDERING THE SHAPE AND DEPTH OF THE
MANTELSCAPE AND THE EFFECTS THAT CAN BE
ACHIEVED. FOR THIS ELEGANT MANTELSCAPE
(RIGHT), HOPPEN CHOOSES A CLASSICAL BUST AS
HER FOCUS, WHICH SHE PLACES OFF-CENTRE.
SHE THEN TAKES SIX LILIES AND PLACES EACH OF
THEM IN A SEPARATE BEAKER, EQUIDISTANT
ALONG THE MANTEL. THE SLANT OF THE FLOWERS
FOLLOWS THE ANGLE OF THE BUST EXACTLY,
PROVIDING AN OVERALL SENSE OF BALANCE,
WHILE THE HORN BEAKERS, RIMMED IN SILVER, ADD
A HIGHLIGHT IN THIS MONOCHROME SCHEME.
FOR A SECOND DISPLAY (FAR RIGHT), HOPPEN
CHOOSES TO ARRANGE HER MANTEL
SYMMETRICALLY. HERE THE ORCHIDS DO NOT
DRAW ATTENTION TO THEMSELVES, RATHER
THEY FRAME THE MIRROR, DRAWING THE EYE IN
TOWARDS THE REFLECTED IMAGE OF THE
BUDDHA. AGAIN, SHE CHOOSES FLOWERS THAT
ARE UNUSUAL AND STRIKING AND THESE
TOO ARE PLANTED IN INDIVIDUAL GLASSES – A
WAY OF DISPLAYING FLOWERS AND PLANTS
THAT PARTICULARLY SUITS THE LONG THIN LINE OF
A MANTELPIECE. THE NEUTRAL BLACK AND
WHITE PALETTE PROVIDES AN EFFECTIVE
BACKGROUND FOR THE LUSTROUS GOLD
OF THE BUDDHA.

a predictable way. Avoiding the obvious is a good design maxim, and when seeking inspiration try to think first about what would be expected in a particular situation, and then think of the opposite. If you expect to see a grand painting or mirror over the fireplace, think how these elements would look elsewhere and what the mantelscape would look like if treated differently.

There is no need to keep rigidly to tradition. Sometimes the mantelscape will be more striking with bare wall above, or you may want to hang something unexpected such as a tribal mask, a textile panel or a lacquered tray. Or instead of one big picture, a tightly packed grouping of four or six smaller pictures may offer a refreshing change. If you do hang a mirror, consider what it will reflect as this offers an ideal opportunity to display a favourite painting or site a piece of sculpture on the opposite wall.

As when furnishing a room, the use of one oversized object in the composition on a mantelscape can create a striking effect. Throw this in as an unexpected surprise – add a disproportionately large candelabra, a Roman bust or some sinuous thin black lamp to a balanced mantelscape and see if it transforms it. A row of oversized single candlesticks, for example, makes a more dramatic statement than two candlesticks placed at either end; they are also a more unconventional choice. On a practical level, using larger objects avoids the over-crowding that results from an arrangement of small decorative items that can end up looking jumbled and disorderly.

Shape and repetition play a large part in giving the display an Eastern feel, the emphasis falling not on the worth of an object but on its pleasing outline. Books, pots and paintbrushes, jars and boxes, bowls and flowers, all have distinctive outlines that can be used in the arranging and balancing of a successful mantelscape. Look at the overall shape of the fireplace itself and see if you can either mirror or counter-balance it in the outlines of the ornaments. There is, for example, a graceful curve in many fireplace insets which is a beautiful feature worth drawing attention to. Equally, a very geometric fireplace will need a dominant curve to balance it out. A fireplace with a great deal of decorative detail may look more effective if treated simply, while a plain stone surround can be an imposing backdrop for a more elaborate set piece. Try it both ways to see which you prefer.

Do not forget that the fireplace goes down to the floor. The arrangement of objects at the foot of a mantelpiece is an unusual and attractive touch, as it is an area that is largely ignored. A tall vase, rounded stones, square boxes or geometric seats, placed either side of the fireplace, will act as a counterbalance to the objects on the mantel, echoing or balancing shapes, or adding an extra dimension of colour or texture. This design trick will serve to draw the viewer's attention to the composition as a whole.

The mantelpiece has always been the traditional resting point for a flower arrangement, usually in a bowl or vase. Flower arranging has been practised for centuries in Japan and China where it has evolved into a highly stylized art form. The type of flower used in Eastern arrangements tends to differ from those used in the West. Exotic orchids, lilies and peonies are particular favourites and create a totally different effect from European flowers like roses or daffodils. Eastern flower arranging uses just one or two blooms to make a statement, and this can be adapted Western-style by using single, striking blooms in an identical row of oversized drinking glasses or sculptural vases. This also takes into account the long, thin shape of a mantelshelf – sometimes a tricky place for a big bowl of flowers.

Remember to take into consideration not only the shape but the colour of your chosen flowers when deciding on what effect you would like to achieve. Do they complement or contrast with the decorative scheme in the room? Do you need to use the mantelscape

THINK ABOUT EACH MANTELSCAPE AS A WHOLE, TAKING INTO CONSIDERATION THE ARRANGEMENT AT THE BASE AS WELL AS THAT ON THE MANTEL ITSELF. THIS DRAMATIC COMPOSITION IS HELD TOGETHER WITH A WARM COLOUR SCHEME OF ORANGES, REDS AND BROWNS, IN WHICH THE COLOURS ORIGINATE FROM THE MATERIALS THEMSELVES: THE HIGHLY POLISHED SHEEN ON THE WOODEN STOOLS AND TRUNK, AND THE VIBRANT ORANGE OF THE GERBERAS. THIS IS A COMPOSITION OF SQUARES AND RECTANGLES, WHERE HOPPEN TAKES THE SQUARE OPENING OF THE FIREPLACE AS HER STARTING POINT. THE TWO STOOLS EITHER SIDE ECHO THIS SHAPE, WHILE THE TRUNK AND PICTURE ADD BALANCE AND VARIETY. THE ARRANGEMENT IS ALSO HIGHLY SYMMETRICAL WITH THE TWO SQUARE STOOLS PLACED EITHER SIDE OF THE MANTELSCAPE, AND THE PICTURE AND TRUNK SITUATED ABOVE AND BELOW. THESE GEOMETRIC FORMS PROVIDE THE STRUCTURE WITHIN WHICH SHE ADDS THE SOFT, CIRCULAR SHAPE OF THE FLOWERS, WHICH ARE PLACED IN A NEAT, SERRIED ROW ALONG THE MANTEL. THESE FLOWERS, IN THEIR COMPACT TERRACOTTA POTS, EXTEND BEYOND THE MANTELPIECE TO THE TRUNK, AND THE USE OF EVEN NUMBERS (TWO STOOLS, EIGHT FLOWERS ALONG THE MANTEL, TWO ON THE TRUNK) THROUGHOUT THE ARRANGEMENT EMPHASIZES THE FORMALITY OF THE DISPLAY.

MANTELSCAPES

LOOK BEYOND THE TRADITIONAL VASE OF
FLOWERS WHEN ARRANGING MANTELSCAPES.
HERE, HOPPEN TAKES AN UNCONVENTIONAL
APPROACH, USING TINS COVERED IN ORIENTAL
NEWSPRINT TO MAKE THE MOST OF A DOZEN
BLOOMS. THE LEAFLESS TWIGS, POKED INTO
A BED OF MOSS, ARE AN UNUSUAL SUBSTITUTE
FOR TRADITIONAL GREENERY. THE RESULT IS
A MORE GRAPHIC OUTLINE AGAINST A PLAIN
WHITE WALL. BULBS ARE THE OBVIOUS CHOICE
FOR THIS KIND OF TREATMENT, BUT DRIED
FLOWERS CAN BE EQUALLY EFFECTIVE AND
OFFER SIMILARLY STRONG OUTLINES. THIS KIND
OF TREATMENT HAS INFINITE VARIATIONS FOR
BOTH CONTAINERS AND PLANTS, AND IS EASY
TO ACHIEVE WITH EFFECTIVE RESULTS.

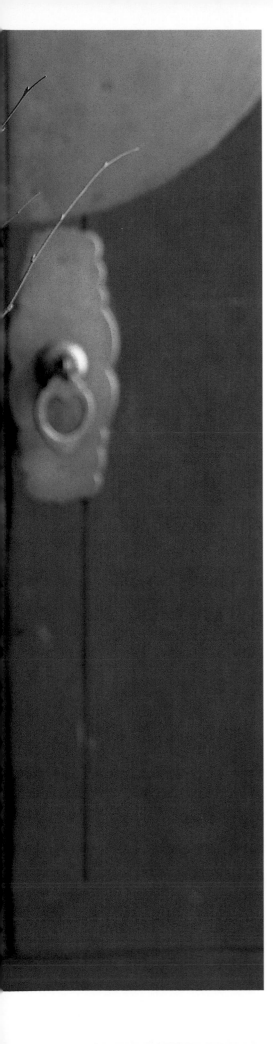

as the focus of the room, or to introduce highlights and accents, or would you prefer to repeat the themes and hues you already have? If you have a dominant colour scheme in a room, experiment with shades from the opposite end of the colour spectrum for your mantelscape: for example, a dash of scarlet in a predominantly green room, or blue china ranged along the mantel in a yellow room. All of these options will work – it is just a question of personal preference. It goes without saying that the other principles discussed in this book all work beautifully in mantelscapes: the use of texture and tonal contrast; always working with a limited palette of shades; the mix of surfaces achieved by using the natural grain of materials; the use of vibrant colour in single dramatic splashes.

As a focal point in a room the mantelscape offers a host of design possibilities and deserves the same care and attention as any other decorative element. Unusual objects and artefacts, combinations of Eastern and Western treasures, will draw the eye and when you get tired of a particular composition it can be changed with the minimum of fuss and expense. There really aren't any rules. Above all, allow the organization of your mantelscape to express both your creativity and individuality.

MANTELSCAPES

TABLESCAPES

KELLY HOPPEN CREATES A PARED-DOWN TABLE-
SCAPE BY MAKING USE OF STRONG COLOURS AND
DEFINITE SHAPES. THE RUNNERS ACROSS
THE TABLE ARE EDGED WITH A CONTRASTING
BORDER AND CRISS-CROSS THE TABLE WITH
GRAPHIC EFFECT, WHILE THE CHOICE OF
ARTICHOKES INSTEAD OF A CONVENTIONAL
FRUITBOWL OR FLOWER ARRANGEMENT PROVIDES
A SCULPTURAL FOCAL POINT. THE WHOLE
SCHEME IS BASED ON CONTRAST
– ROUND AND SQUARE, LIGHT AND DARK – AND
KNOTTED FORTUNY NAPKINS AND
SCENTED CANDLES SOFTEN THE SETTING.

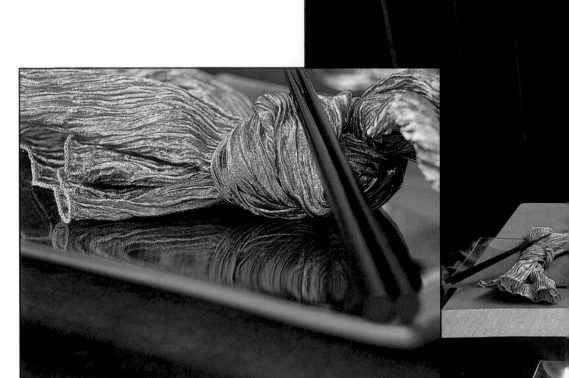

The art of display is particularly strong throughout Asia, especially when applied to table-scapes and the display of food. The line-up of produce in any shop window or market stall will demonstrate an instinctive understanding of shape, form and colour. A tray of brightly coloured sweets in Japan, a market trader's trolley of green vegetables in India or the beautifully balanced harmonies of a dish in a Chinese restaurant are all a pleasure to the eye. Once again, the basic principles of order and harmony, of *yin* and *yang*, of repetition and balance underlie each arrangement, and are adopted and developed in the East meets West style. In the East, particular skill is employed when arranging numerous objects in a small space, and this is accomplished with a compactness that ruthlessly excludes anything extraneous. The tea-ceremony room, measured out in *tatami* mats, has a place for everything, and everything is perfectly in its place. Each element is functional and each action is carried out with precision, an attitude which can be usefully adapted in Western tablescapes.

The objects themselves are important, too. From the hand-beaten engraved silver of Thailand and the lacquerware of Burma to the ceramics of China, the brass cookware of India and the *sake* cups and tea bowls of Japan, there are endless beautiful things which, if arranged sympathetically on a tabletop, will give an East-West feeling to a room without any further decoration. Many items come in sets – opium weights in the shape of small carved animals are common throughout Asia, and in Japan the belt toggles,

REPETITION IS THE KEY TO ALL KELLY HOPPEN'S TABLESCAPES, AND ODD NUMBERS CAN BE EFFECTIVE FOR LESS FORMAL SCHEMES. A CAREFULLY THOUGHT-OUT TABLESCAPE CAN ADD THE FINISHING TOUCHES TO A ROOM WHEN THE FINAL RESULT IS NOT INTENDED FOR A FORMAL MEAL. FOR EXAMPLE, THESE THREE AMARYLLIS BULBS (LEFT) IN IDENTICAL POTS PROVIDE AN ESSENTIAL SPLASH OF VIVID COLOUR IN A ROOM THAT IS OTHERWISE PLAIN AND UNDERSTATED. THIS EFFECT COULD BE REPEATED WITH ALMOST ANY KIND OF FLOWER, BUT HOPPEN PREFERS THOSE THAT HAVE UNUSUAL SHAPES – LILIES, ORCHIDS AND TULIPS – AND BOLD COLOURS. ATTENTION TO DETAIL IS ESSENTIAL, AND EVEN THE FLOWER POTS HAVE BEEN CONSIDERED. THESE TERRACOTTA FLOWER POTS, PLEASANTLY AGED AND FILLED WITH MOSS, COMPLEMENT THE NEUTRAL COLOUR SCHEME OF THE ROOM. A TABLESCAPE DOES NOT NEED TO BE LARGE-SCALE, IN FACT, THE ORCHESTRATION OF SMALL OBJECTS CAN BE EQUALLY EYE-CATCHING AND PREVENTS THEM FROM APPEARING AS CLUTTER. THE INTRINSIC BEAUTY OF POLISHED AND LACQUERED WOOD (RIGHT) IS ALLOWED TO SPEAK FOR ITSELF WITHOUT ANY OTHER VISUAL DISTRACTIONS. THE RICH REDS AND BROWNS OF THE OPIUM CONTAINERS ECHO THE TONES OF THE WOODEN BOX AND TABLE. SIMILAR HARMONIES CAN BE ACHIEVED USING A VARIETY OF DIFFERENT THEMES SUCH AS STONE OR IRON.

TABLESCAPES

A RICH LEAF GREEN IS COMBINED WITH A SMART BLACK TO CREATE A STYLISH, FORMAL TABLE SETTING BASED ON CONTRASTING SHAPES. SUCH SETTINGS CAN OFTEN LOOK CONFUSED, BUT A DISCIPLINED USE OF COLOUR HAS A CALMING INFLUENCE. THE LARGE CIRCULAR CELADON CHARGERS AND EVEN THE CENTREPIECE – THICK, TROPICAL GREEN LEAVES ARRANGED IN PAPIER-MÂCHÉ OFFERING BOWLS FROM THAILAND – MANAGE TO LOOK LAVISH YET RESTRAINED.

or *netsuke*, carved like miniature sculptures and used to tie a kimono, are now very collectable. Lacquerware and basketry also come in tiered sizes and blue-and-white ceramics are a dominant theme throughout Japan and China, while stone, wood and gold leaf are favoured materials. It is not necessary to have wholly Eastern collections either – a shape, colour or material will often have echoes in a similar European item – rice bowls with handmade slipware, or a Thai silver bowl with a Georgian candlestick. Sometimes there will be similarities in the simplicity of two objects, at other times it will be their ornateness that draws them together, even if they are made in different materials and have different functions.

The East-West tablescape is based on a subtle mixture of repetition and balance. Probably the simplest way of creating a tablescape is to take one object – a leather book, a ginger jar, a silver spoon, a *netsuke* or an opium weight – and repeat it, either in several neat rows or in an apparently spontaneous grouping. This is a simple device, and one that works anywhere. It is particularly effective when the objects themselves are striking – a line of brilliant flowers down the centre of a table, a row of blue-and-white ginger jars or a display of elaborate Indian brass.

Alternatively, you can choose just one element and repeat it. This could be the colour – blue and white, celadon green, or Chinese red; or it could be a material, such as leather, silver or wood; or a motif, such as a flower. A stylized flower pattern on a curtain might sit beside a table holding a vase of real flowers and a box inlaid with a mother-of-pearl flower motif. Shape can also be used successfully as a repetitive theme:

TABLESCAPES

OLD BOOKS, WITH THEIR WORN VELLUM COVERS, ARE ALWAYS A PLEASURE TO SEE AND FEEL, AND HERE HOPPEN ECHOES THE SHAPES OF THE SOFA CUSHIONS BY SCATTERING A COLLECTION OF ANTIQUE BOOKS ACROSS THE TABLE IN FRONT OF THE SOFA. SHAPE IS ALSO THE KEY TO THE PLACING OF THIS SIAMESE HEAD (LEFT), A CIRCULAR PLATE AND A SQUARE LACQUERED BOX REFLECTING THE SHAPE OF THE SCULPTURE.

a circular tray with three different sizes of circular bowl placed on it, or four different kinds of square jar ranged in a row. Shapes can also be more subtly linked: a conical sculpture and a shallow bowl might echo each other without being exact replicas.

The oriental principle of balancing a display is one which can be adapted beautifully to tablescapes. Here the principles of *yin* and *yang* can be invoked to help understand it. *Yin* and *yang* equate to round and straight, dark and light, cold and warm. Two round bowls and a square jar make a balanced composition. Three boxes need their squareness rounded off with a collection of round stone balls in a bowl. A collection of dark wood and lacquerwork is highlighted by a single pale rose. Even when some of the items themselves are quite intricate, these arrangements offer simplicity and harmony.

One of the many pleasures in having a beautifully designed home is being able to share it with family and friends, and a meal offers an ideal occasion to bring a number of people together in your home. The East meets West style is a look that takes into consideration the smallest detail, and the arrangement of a dinner table and the food being served is as important in an interiors scheme as the arrangement of your furnishings. This attention to detail provides the final touches for a total look.

The culinary influence of the Pacific Rim countries has been one of the most exciting developments in cooking and eating. Eastern spices like ginger, cardamom and star anise meet Western ingredients in homes and restaurants around the world. Eastern styles of cooking, such as stir-frying and steaming, work with more traditional Western methods, such as boiling and grilling. With all this interest in oriental ingredients has come

TABLESCAPES

TWO WAYS OF TREATING A FORMAL DINNER
PARTY: THE INTRICATELY CARVED WOODEN TABLE
(RIGHT) IS LEFT UNCOVERED FOR ALL TO ENJOY.
SILK RIBBON NAPKIN HOLDERS PROVIDE A
TEXTURAL CONTRAST (HOPPEN CUTS THEM
EXTRA LONG) WHILE LARGE PLATES, OR
CHARGERS, ARE USED TO PROTECT THE WOOD.
ALTERNATIVELY, A DIFFERENT APPROACH
MIGHT BE CALLED FOR WITH CRISP WHITE
LINEN NAPKINS CONTRASTING WITH THE DARK
TARTAN TABLECLOTH WHICH ANCHORS THE
SCHEME (ABOVE). FLOWERS AND CANDLES ARE
A FAVOURITE WITH HOPPEN, PLACED ON THE
TABLE OR AROUND THE ROOM – NOTE THE
STRIKING ARRANGEMENT OF TWIGS AND THE
CANDLES ADORNING THE MANTELPIECE.
THE RESULT IS A 'TOTAL LOOK' FOR THE ROOM.

a fresh look at the way food is presented. Even the humblest workman's lunch in Japan is exquisitely arranged, with a careful balance of shapes and colours to equal the most prestigious restaurants of the West. There is now a new awareness of the tablescape, whether for formal entertaining or a supper for friends. The total effect should appeal to all the senses, and this starts with the laying of the table.

Although the final result can look quite elaborate, simple shapes and plain colours are the building blocks of table decoration East-West style. Big round plates may be earthenware, porcelain or glass but they are pulled together with a colour theme: jade or celadon green, or a rich oriental blue. Clear or coloured glass picks up the theme and repeats it. The use of chargers, or giant plates, instead of table mats has become popular in restaurants and homes in the West. Give the look an Eastern twist by borrowing lotus or banana leaves from the markets, and using them as a substitute for the top plate. The table itself should be linear or square wherever possible (square tables concentrate energy while round tables spin energy off, according to Chinese tradition), but the decorative elements used within the arrangement can interconnect through a circular theme: the shape of the plates, glasses, vases or even the tubular shapes of flowers.

Table decoration is kept monochrome for maximum effectiveness with a clever use of shape and texture. For the centrepiece, try to avoid arrangements that are predictable or conventional. For a bowl of flowers, select exotic blooms with unusual shapes – maybe the tall slender form of orchids or the shorter rounder form of tulips – or opt for a potted plant instead. Alternatively, arrange a pile of sculptural artichokes in a bowl, or create an arrangement of glossy dark green leaves. This is a style that can be adapted to any striking colour or interesting shape, such as a pile of citrussy limes or squashes. Napkins run with the colour theme, but often have a contrasting texture – pleated Fortuny napkins or scrunchy linen ones.

As a final touch, the Eastern banner treatment can also be used to smarten up tables, giving order to place settings as on a grid, and giving definition and impact to china and glass. Try a runner of upholstery scrim, linen, richly coloured velvet or even brocade along the centre of the table. It looks equally good against either bare wood or over a tablecloth. An overlapping cruciform arrangement can be left simple or layered. Using these few, basic design directives, a huge range of tablescapes can be composed to give a different look for a different occasion.

TABLESCAPES

AUTHOR'S ACKNOWLEDGMENTS

Special thanks to all my clients who allowed me back into their homes to photograph, without them this book would not have been possible. The unfailing help and cooperation of John Carter at The Flower Van, Guinevere Antiques and Snapdragon was also greatly appreciated.

I would like to acknowledge my stylist Arabella McNie who was an invaluable help to me whilst photographing this book.

Also, great thanks go to Ricca who has been a constant support.

SPECIAL PHOTOGRAPHY CREDITS

Photographer: Bill Batten
Assistant to the photographer: Giles Westley
Stylist: Arabella McNie

The author would like to thank the following who supplied material for photography: Alexandre Armstrong; Andrew Martin; Bentley's; Besselink and Jones; Bill Amberg; The Conran Shop; De La Cuona; The General Trading Company; Habitat; The Holding Company; Muji; Nicholas Haslam; Nina Campbell; Pauline Thomas; Pierre Frey; The Room; Selfridges; Thomas Goode; Valerie Wade; William Yeoward.

PUBLISHER'S ACKNOWLEDGMENTS

Conran Octopus would like to thank the following photographers and organizations for their permission to reproduce the photographs in this book:

4 Carlos Navajas/The Image Bank; 6–7 Noelle Höeppe; 8–9 Andreas von Einsiedel; 10 below Tony Souter/The Hutchinson Library; 11 above Carlos Navajas/The Image Bank; 12 Andrew Wood; 14 below Carlos Navajas/The Image Bank; 14 left Alvis Upitit/The Image Bank; 15 below right Carlos Navajas/The Image Bank; 16 above & below left Carlos Navajas/The Image Bank; 18 above left Carlos Navajas/The Image Bank; 18 below left Lisi Dennis/The Image Bank; 20 left Carlos Navajas/The Image Bank; 20 right Zefa Pictures; 22 above left Barbazza/Marka; 22 below left Carlos Navajas/The Image Bank 23 centre Carlos Navajas/The Image Bank; 24 left Christine Osbourne Pictures; 30 right Carlos Navajas/The Image Bank; 32 left Zefa Pictures; 35 Carlos Navajas/The Image Bank; 37 J. Ch. Gerard/Diaf; 38 right Carlos Navajas/The Image Bank; 40–1 Paul Ryan/International Interiors; 42 Shin Kimura (from *Japan Country Living, Spirit-Tradition-Style*, ©1993 Charles E. Tuttle Company); 45 Roy Lewis; 48 below David Silverberg/Impact; 51 right Helene Rogers/Trip; 52 left Carlos Navajas/The

Image Bank; 55 right Paul Ryan/International Interiors; 57 left & right Paul Ryan/International Interiors; 58 above Jim Holmes/Axiom Photographic Agency; 60 right Carlos Navajas/The Image Bank; 64–5 Roy Lewis; 65 Jim Holmes/Axiom Photographic Agency; 67 right John Lewis/The Image Bank; 69 right Lisi Dennis/The Image Bank; 70 left A. Perigot (stylist: J.P. Billaud)/Marie Claire Maison; 70 below David Black Oriental Carpets; 75 right Don Klumpp/The Image Bank; 78 left John Biglow Taylor; 80 Carlos Navajas/The Image Bank; 82 left Carlos Navajas/The Image Bank; 84 Carlos Navajas/The Image Bank; 86–7 Ray Main; 90 David Wade/Mega Press; 97 Carlos Navajas/The Image Bank; 99 Roy Lewis; 100 Carlos Navajas/The Image Bank; 102 Andreas von Einsiedel/Elizabeth Whiting & Associates; 104 right Carlos Navajas/The Image Bank; 107 right Gille de Chabaneix (from *Japanese Style*, by Suzanne Slesin, Stafford Cliff & Daniel Rozensztroch); 113 Zefa Pictures; 116 left Shin Kimura (from *Japan Country Living, Spirit-Tradition-Style*, ©1993 Charles E. Tuttle Company); 118–119 Carlos Navajas/The Image Bank; 120–1 David Black Oriental Carpets; 129 above right Carlos Navajas/The Image Bank; 132 Mulberry Home; 136 above centre Carlos Navajas/The Image Bank; 156 Fritz von der Schulenburg/The Interior Archive; 156–157 Andrew Wood

ACKNOWLEDGMENTS